GUIDED MEDITATION FOR M… SS AND … N:

HOW AND TO CHANGE AND CALM YOUR MIND. STRESS FREE WITH SELF HEALING. UNDERSTANDING AND PRACTICING BUDDHISM. YOGA AND ZEN MADE PLAIN FOR BEGINNERS

"PEACE OF SOUL AND BRAIN" FOUNDATION

TABLE OF CONTENTS

Introduction

Meditation is the way to quieten the mind for a bit. It is a simple activity that can give you better control over your mind and your thoughts. You will be able to practically empty your mind for some time and then refill it with positive things. The time you get through meditation helps you in objectively selecting the thoughts you want to work on. You can single out each and every negative thought in your mind and choose to discard it forever. Meditation can give you great control over the thought process and effectively over your life.

It can prove to be an effective cure of the sorrows, fears, anxieties, feelings of hatred and general confusion that plague your life. It is one of the best ways to completely transform the mind. You will be able to achieve a state of thoughtless awareness. This will not only make your mind clear but also relaxed and inwardly focused.

Meditation is the way to understand the cause of the problems plaguing the mind. It is the deep state of thought where you are able to view things objectively and make a better judgment.

The best thing about meditation is that you don't need anything extra to do all this. You only need to sit, stand, or walk quietly. Once you get fairly acquainted with the process you can do it anywhere. You will have amazing control over your life and would be able to feel the bliss you have been longing for. You'll become more joyful, satisfied, and peaceful.

Modern life has become a race in which we all are running without a goal. In this race, no one can be victorious as there is no finish line. Meditation will give you the required understanding to enjoy the race.

You'll be learning everything you need to know from learning how to be aware of the present moment to learning how to become aware of your own thoughts and feelings. These are important building blocks to meditation as often time we don't want to take the time for ourselves. Many of us spend a good chunk of time worrying about others and trying to get as much done as possible. In fact, I would bet that as you read this introduction, you may be holding your breath trying to get to the next point. Take a moment to release that breath, inhale deeply, and try to calm your mind.

As you'll soon be learning, meditation is not about rushing to the next task. As we work our way through several different meditations, I want you to remind yourself that this is not a selfish practice. Much like we nourish our bodies with nutritious foods, it's important to give your mind some peace and quiet. Peace for the soul is just as important as health for the body. When you put both aspects together, you'll be granted the gift of life as you have never experienced before.

Once we have gone over the benefits of meditation and how to create the perfect environment for your practice, you'll learn how to begin your first meditation in chapter four. Here, you'll learn some basic induction skills and how to get the most out of your practice. From breathing exercises to a full-body scan, we'll make sure you are comfortable before furthering your practice into the visualization meditation scripts.

It should be noted that you should not enter this practice with any expectations. The most important factor is that you are taking steps to help relieve your stress and anxiety. There will be moments of frustration when you are unable to quiet the chatter of your brain, but I promise that as you practice more, you'll be able to enjoy the benefits meditation can bring into your life.

Chapter 1

What You Should Know About Hypnosis?

Hypnosis is susceptibility of the mind to suggestions. Despite this state, a person under hypnosis subconsciously knows what is being done except that he/she allows these things to happen.

A common application of hypnosis is hypnotherapy, which aims at improving a well-being. You cannot inflict damage to a person in a hypnotized state. Even in such a state, a person can react to danger. The mind has defense mechanisms that are hard to understand.

The practice of hypnosis has been around for so many centuries. Lately, scientists devote time to study and explain how and why it is possible. Many theories arise regarding the different practices of hypnosis. Here are the truths about hypnosis.

Hypnosis is a natural, inherent trait.

It happens to everyone, in some form or another. You may not recognize it or may even deny that you witness at least once or maybe more. Every person may drift in and out of the hypnosis state.

For example, you are reading a novel. You are so engrossed with the story you do not "hear" your significant other asking you a question. Your conscious mind may not register the question, but you know you are being asked. In some way, it resembles hypnosis. Others do not call it that way.

Since it is a natural trait, a hypnotized person is not at risk of getting stuck in one state or another. They naturally drift to wake state or deep sleep. Thus, hypnosis is not dangerous. The experience is like listening to a boring speech and zoning out until the speaker finishes. Some may feel disoriented, but such feelings do not last.

Hypnosis is not a sleep state.

Although the word hypnosis comes from the Greek word, Hypnos, which means sleep, it does not constitute the normal sleep state. Hypnosis state seems like you are asleep, but your mind is aware, awake and responsive. You hear everything. Your senses heighten.

Hypnosis does not make a person weak-willed.

A hypnotized person is susceptible to suggestions, but it does not mean they are weak-willed. They remain in control. In fact, they can stop hypnosis anytime they want. If hypnosis makes a person weak-willed, hypnotists could abuse such power over a hypnotized person. A lot of hypnotists could command a person to do everything they say. Fortunately, a hypnotized person remains in control despite his/her highly susceptibility to suggestions.

Relaxation is not a prerequisite to hypnosis.

You can hypnotize a person anywhere, anytime, provided that person is willing. You may even do it during a strenuous activity. Hypnosis can bring relaxation, but relaxation is not a prerequisite.

Hypnosis does not cause permanent amnesia.

A hypnotist can command a person to forget, for the time being, what has transpired. This allows the mind to process the events subconsciously. In the long run, a hypnotized person can remember of the hypnosis in great detail.

Hypnosis is different from a trance state.

Many hypnotists have difficulty identifying the difference between hypnotic and trance state. Most of the times, these two words are used interchangeably. The only similarities between the two are the heightened senses and highly efficient mind.

Hypnosis deals with heightened susceptibility of the mind, most likely the subconscious part. Trance state targets both the conscious and subconscious.

Concept of Hypnosis

The human mind is a complex mechanism. Learning these concepts enables you to hypnotize anyone, anytime. Understanding these hypnosis concepts helps you recognize which technique to use.

Power of Suggestion

Sometimes, people act based on someone else's suggestions. This power of suggestion is what advertisers use to convince consumers to buy a product. Hypnotists also use this power of suggestion to induce hypnosis.

The most common example of the power of suggestion is the placebo effect. This is a suggestion during the waking state. Doctors, nurses, pharmacists apply this power of suggestion to patients. The doctors would sometimes give an ordinary pill to patients. Believing that this pill cures their diseases, the patients feel better. Why? The doctors suggested that the particular pill can heal them.

Combined with the power of language, the power of suggestion creates expectations. It creates a powerful way of making the hypnotized person's move towards his or her dominant thoughts.

Power of Imagination

The human mind is capable of unlimited imagination. Together with the power of suggestion, you can create endless possibilities with your hypnosis.

Visualization scripts include the power of imagination. This power helps people achieve something or anything close to their physical limitations or beyond their normal capabilities.

Conscious vs. the Subconscious

In psychology, the mind can function on conscious and subconscious levels. The conscious part is what you can control. The conscious mind makes decisions, thinks logically, and performs cognitive functions. It is the origin of willpower and the recorder of short-term memory. It dwells in the past, present and the future.

On the other hand, the subconscious mind controls body functions and automatic reactions and reflexes. It does not think in executing an action. Like a computer program, once hitting the run button, the subconscious automatically executes whatever actions a body part or organ has to do. Examples are breathing and blinking.

The subconscious mind is the seat of habit and long-term memory. It does not change so easily. Embedded memories, actions, and reactions in the subconscious take time (or years) for newer ones to replace them. The subconscious controls self-preservation mechanisms. This is the reason hypnotists cannot make a person to something bad while hypnotized.

The mind generalizes and filters events, actions, objects or anything seen, felt, heard, tasted, and experienced. Generalization is the ability of the mind to think in blocks or concepts. It makes thinking quicker especially in times of danger. Filtering is the ability to block sensory inputs and delete negative mental images.

Language Patterns

Hypnotists use language patterns to hypnotize other people. These patterns include dissociation, supposition, double binds, metaphors, embedded commands, exploration, and anticipation.

Use of Metaphors

Metaphorical language pattern is an excellent way to make other people trust you. They can relate to what you are saying without the feeling of intrusion to their personal lives. With metaphors, you can speak about the lives of your targets and still be confident that you can hypnotize them.

Double Binds

This language pattern offers choices, usually two, to your subjects or targets. Whatever the answer is, the outcome is the same. Most of the time double binds language pattern is only answerable with a yes or no.

Embedded Commands

In this language pattern, you are commanding other people do what you want them to do. It is usually used in an authoritarian method of inducing hypnosis. However, scrutinizing closely induction scripts, all induction techniques, except non-verbal method, use embedded commands to deliver suggestions and ask permissions.

Dissociation

This pattern uses an out of the body experience. Many people fall into a dissociation state when they experience stress and traumatic events.

This dissociation seems to be a natural response of most people. Dissociation happens naturally during hypnosis. You can utilize this natural occurrence to hypnotize other people.

The Laws of the Mind

Thoughts affect the body. If the mind thinks you are strong, the body seems to follow. This is the reason constant emotional stress weakens the body. You can use this law to induce hypnosis. If your targets think that hypnosis is possible, they are more susceptible than those people who are skeptical.

Concentrated attention

The more you think of something, the more it becomes a reality. For an instance, constant, repeated imagination of wanting to become more sociable or efficient in work will make your conscious mind believe it. As a result, you find ways to achieve it.

However, for people who have difficulty separating between reality and imagination, concentrated attention has a negative effect. These people sometimes live in a world of protected cocoon.

In hypnosis, you can use this law of the mind to hypnotize anyone and strengthen your suggestions to your subjects. Concentrated attention makes your targets believe in anything you suggest them to do.

Dominant effect

People create habit over time. They hold on to this habit to rationalize behavior and thoughts. Once an idea is embedded in the mind, it takes time for this to be replaced a new one. For new ideas to replace old ones, people need strong emotional connection or consequences.

Association

The opposite of dissociation, people sometimes feel when they can relate such emotions with something. For example, classical music relaxes the mind while metal rock music evokes harsh and negative vibes.

Reverse Effect

This law proposes that the conscious mind cannot force the subconscious to follow. The greater is the effort of the conscious mind to understand or remember something the harder it is for the subconscious to response.

Negation

The mind does not know how to compute negation. When you say do not think of this or that, the first thing the mind does is to think of this or that. For example, do not imagine that this elephant is colored in violet. The mind interprets it as "see the elephant, it is violet."

Compounding

This law utilizes the compounding effect of repeated suggestions. Every time you make same suggestions over and over again to the same person with only slight variations, you are creating a pattern. On the succeeding hypnosis, induction is easier than the first to third sessions.

Core Beliefs

Core beliefs are created early in life. These beliefs determine who you are and what you are in life. However, every core belief does not define all aspects of your life. One core belief may define how you deal with your social life but not how you manage your work environment.

These core beliefs are consistent with the rest of your life but can be altered through hypnosis, will power and by other life changing events. These beliefs play a big role in retaining long term problems in your life.

Understanding these personal core beliefs will help you in knowing exactly how to hypnotize anyone.

Chapter 2
Relaxation Techniques

Technique 1: Meditation

When the body and mind are stressed, you need to slow down. It is best to commence a relaxation response. Studies have shown that daily meditation and prayer not only eases one's anxiety, but it also helps modify the neural pathways of the brain making it more resistant to stress.

You should practice meditation and prayer every single day, especially during stressful situations. It will help you focus on better things and keep your mind off stressful conditions. When your mind is relaxed and focused, you can go back to challenges and obstacles with a clear thought and course of action. Even if you will not be able to solve the stressful situation you are facing now, meditation will keep your body from releasing bad hormones that can damage your health.

Mindful meditation is important when quieting your mind. It is the art of becoming heedful or attentive to your thoughts and feelings, your surroundings and your bodily responses.

Reducing stress levels may be the first benefit when you meditate. It has long-term effects such as increased self-awareness and lesser bouts of depression. You will find that you will easily be content with life, you will be more confident with yourself and stressful situations will not bother you as much in the future.

A simple meditation exercise you can try today is to simply sit in a comfortable position and focus your attention on your breathing. You don't need to alter your breathing in any way, simply focus on it. Your mind will wander many times, each time it does, simply forgive yourself and have some humor about it, and return to your breathing.

Technique 2: Relaxed Breathing

You can practice the art of breathing deeply at regular intervals, which will calm and soothe you deeply. This will help improve the air and blood circulation in the body and produce calming effects.

You need to make yourself feel comfortable.

Here are some things you can do:

- Go to a quiet place with less distractions.

- Loosen tight clothing or remove your shoes, jewelry and jacket.

- Get a comfortable chair that will support your head. Make sure that your arms are placed on the arm rest and your feet are firmly planted on the ground. You should not cross your legs.

- You can also lie on a bed or on the floor. Place your arms away from your body with your palms facing up. Stretch your legs out making sure they are apart.

Once you are comfortable enough, you can now focus on your breathing. To start, inhale and exhale slowly in a regular beat or rhythm.

Technique 3: Laugh Out Loud

Laughter is the best medicine is such an old saying but still rings true. It is no joke that laughter is one of the best techniques for stress relief. Chuckles and chortles, giggles and guffaws – they may not cure all illnesses, but they sure can lighten your load.

So go ahead and try to laugh. Even if it is forced, laughter can do wonders to your body and mind. Turn up your mouth and smile and start with a chuckle. You will feel that your body will be less tensed, and you will feel lighter.

Technique 4: Improve Your Sense Of Humor

Having a positive outlook will help you deal with stressful situations effectively. Having a good sense of humor will increase your chances of getting over something stressful quickly.

Finding something humorous in your own situation and laughing about it will help you fight stress. It will do your body good to chuckle in the face of challenges.

If you feel that you don't have a funny bone in your body, don't fret. You can learn to have humor and it can be developed.

When you are trying to be funny, it is important to exercise discretion. There are some things that aren't meant to be laughed at. There are forms of humor that is out of place and hurtful such as laughing at the expense of other people. So always be socially intelligent, which I'm sure you are.

Laughing with your friends and family is especially bonding. If you find yourself alone a great deal, try to take some time to watch or read something funny. The effects of humor are amazing and can-do wonders for your spirit and counter stress very quickly. Research has shown that using humor to respond to stress can help you live longer by an average of four years!

Technique 5: Decompress

If you are feeling stressed, your body will tense up and your muscles will become sore. You can feel this particularly on your neck and shoulders. There will be a heavy feeling as if you are literally carrying a weight.

To soothe the muscle tension, you can use a warm compress or heat wrap. Place it around your shoulders and neck.

After you put the warm compress around the tensed muscles, close your eyes to relax. Sit or lie down in a way that your neck, chest, back muscles and face will be relaxed. The heat from the wrap will cause your muscles to loosen up. After 10 minutes, you can gently massage the muscles on your neck and shoulders to ease the tension. It is best if someone can do it for you so you will not strain your arm muscles.

Technique 6: Eat Stress Busting Foods

Foods can relieve stress in different ways. There are comfort foods that improve the levels of serotonin in your brain. It has a calming effect on the body. Other foods help lower the levels of adrenaline and cortisol to counter the effects of stress.

You need to have a healthy diet so that your body becomes strong enough to combat stress, improve your immune system and lower your blood pressure. And you need to know which foods to eat when you are in a stressful situation, so help your body fight off stress and not add to it.

Technique 7: Exercise

You can change your diet or munch on stress busting foods to relieve your stress, but it will also help if you get moving and start exercising. If you are not active, chances are, stress eating will make you overweight.

When you move your body, you increase the circulation of oxygen in your blood and help your brain release endorphins.

You do not need to be too athletic, but it is best to do some aerobic exercises at least three times a week for 30 minutes. You can do all kinds of exercises as well such as walking, jogging, biking and yoga to help ease your anxiety. You can walk up and down the stairs and do some stretching as well.

Technique 8: Incorporate Music In Your Life

Integrate music into your life to help you blow off your steam. Music can lower your heart rate and blood pressure and help decrease your anxiety. Music has the power to soothe your soul because it has a unique and effective link to your emotions.

You need to create a playlist of songs that will help you focus and relax. Slow, classical music is known to have a calming effect, but different people have different preferences. The choice of music is really up to you. It can be nature sounds or different melodies and instruments. It can be a variety of songs and singers. It can even be upbeat tunes.

Music will help distract your attention away from stressful situations and quiet your mind. It is a good aid when you are meditating. When your mind is relaxed and focused on things that are not stressful, you can be effective at finding solutions to what you are facing. You can explore your emotions so you can better deal with situations at hand.

Technique 9: Reach Out And Relate

We may have saved the best for last. Just as you physically reach out during an exercise or internally reach out during meditation and listening to music, reaching out and relating to other people will help you deal with your stress levels.

Your social network is a great tool for managing stress and it this doesn't mean social media. It is not about ranting on Facebook or Twitter. It is more than posting your emotions on a mood board. It is about actually relating to people.

Talking with others will help your mind relax and sort things out. It can be done face-to-face, or it can be done over the phone. You can pour out your emotions and share your problems with family and friends.

Technique 10: An Attitude Of Gratitude

There are people who can deal with just about anything and still stay happy. They can enjoy the good times and tough it out during the bad. Their focus is on the positive side of everything and they always see the best in people and situations.

To be able to maintain a positive outlook in life, it is vital that you appreciate what you have. When you have an attitude of gratitude – a thankful spirit – then you will not be beaten down by any storm or stressful situation. Emotional resilience can be improved by gratitude.

You can cultivate this attitude regardless of your personality or temperament. With a little practice, you can go from stress to optimism and maintain a good mood. Think about what you have now and be thankful. Do not compare what you have with what others have.

Do not worry about tomorrow's concerns or yesterday's regrets. Live in the present. Be grateful for the little things and the big things in your life. Meditate on the goodness of God in your life, His blessings and favors upon you. When challenges come, be grateful that you have the ability to overcome it or that you have friends who can help you go through it.

People who have a grateful attitude develop stringer relationships and are generally happy. They have a greater sense of purpose in life and become content.

Positivity will help lower cortisol levels that cause your body to feel anxious. And positivity comes when you are grateful. With gratefulness, you live life with more purpose, you appreciate the people around you, the job that you have, the roof above your head and all the other things that are part of your life. You will live happier, sleep better and be healthier.

Gratitude will help you stay focused on all that's good in your life and stop the stressful habit of ruminating on all your worries. Keep a gratitude journal (but don't stress about getting it perfect and writing in there every day!) and write in there one or two things you're grateful for, once or twice a week.

Chapter 3

Causes of Anxiety And Panic Attacks

Understanding anxiety and panic attacks can't be complete without looking at the causes. The aim is to ensure that we treat the root cause of anxiety and not just focus on symptoms. Understanding the cause of anxiety makes it possible for us to address the issues related to the conditions. There are two broad causes of anxiety

I) External Causes

II) Internal Causes

External causes mainly refer to daily life circumstances that may lead to pressure. The external causes of anxiety may be social or environmental. These causes may lead to anxiety and panic attacks all alike. The internal cause of anxiety refers to factors that you may have control over. These are inbuilt emotions and ideas that may lead to anxiety.

External Causes of Anxiety

- Stress at work and Stress from school: Social stress imposed on a person by work and school expectations may lead to anxiety. Although this is not common, it happens. If a person feels that they may lose their job or fail in their exams, they may start experiencing anxiety. It is important to learn and handle the job pressure. If things are not working well at your workplace, you need to find a way of handling the situation. Poor management of stressful situations will in one way or another lead to anxiety or panic attacks. If you cannot talk with your boss or explain your situation to another employee, the pressure might get to your head leading to constant fear, worry, and intense nervousness even in a situation where there is no alarm.

- Stress in a personal relationship: Stress from personal relationships such as marriage, courtship, and friendship may also lead to anxiety. This is very common for individuals who are in abusive relationships. Narcissistic abuse victims are known to suffer from anxiety and panic attacks many years after getting out of such relationships. If you realize that a close friend is showing any of the above symptoms after getting into a new relationship, you have the responsibility to help him/her. You should help such a person get out of an abusive relationship or at least, make them open about the situation. If a person who is in a stressful relationship speaks out, he/she may be able to find the needed help. In most cases, individuals who are in stressful relationships lose their sobriety. Their thinking gets clouded by the relationship. They are unable to make decisions or choices that are beneficial for their life and are vulnerable to more abuse. External help from friends and family may go a long way in helping such individuals.

- Financial stress: Lack of finances is also another situation that may drive a person to the wall. This often occurs to men, who are deemed as breadwinners in most families. If a person feels that they are being devalued due to a lack of money, they may plunge into depression. It is important for all of us to be watchful and helpful of any individuals who may be suffering from financial stress. Such individuals can be helped via financial counseling and financial advice.

- Stress from an emotional trauma such as the death of a loved one: This is a common cause of anxiety and panic attacks. If you lose someone so close to you, it may take long before you attain full healing. Individuals who have lost dear family members have to spend a lot of time thinking about their past experiences with their loved ones. They are constantly lost in their thoughts thinking about the good times they shared with their loved ones. It is important to ensure that we all pay close attention to friends who suffer such loses. If we can stay close and show love to such individuals, it is easy for them to heal and recover from the psychological trauma. For such individuals, they only suffer due to denial. Refusing to come to terms with reality and living in a false world may cause a victim of such traumatic events to stay in anxiety for a long time. However, if the victims can be helped to come to terms with the occurrences, healing is easily achieved.

- Stress from a serious medical illness: Medical conditions can cause stress and anxiety to some people too. This is common when a person is diagnosed with a chronic condition. Some diseases are associated with death or excruciating pain. It is also such diseases that are associated with stigma. For instance, individuals diagnosed with cancer or HIV are likely to suffer from anxiety. If you realize that a person who is close has been diagnosed by such conditions, the best solution is to offer a helping hand. Most people diagnosed with chronic conditions end up dying not because they were unable to handle the condition but because of stigma. If you can keep your friends who suffer from deep conditions close, you may help reduce anxiety and panic attacks.

- Side Effects of Drugs: There is no doubt about the fact that some drugs affect the normal functioning of the brain. If you are undergoing medication, your body must experience changes. The same applies to anxiety. Some drugs may cause nervousness and anxiety. Some of the common drugs that may cause anxiety include alcohol, caffeine, and cocaine among others. The same case applies to some prescription medicinal drugs such as Ritalin and amphetamines. These drugs may lead a person to feel light-headed and as a result, lead to panic attacks and anxiety.

- Symptoms of medical illness: Individuals who have suffered from panic attacks are always afraid of suffering from the same. This may lead to fear and constant worry, especially if the patient suffers from illnesses such as stroke and heart attack. Since the symptoms of heart diseases are like panic attacks, the patients of such diseases may suffer panic attacks when the symptoms of the illness show up.

- Lack of oxygen in circumstances as diverse as high altitude: Oxygen or lack of it may lead to panic attacks. When a person is in a place where there is no enough supply of oxygen, the breathing mechanism of the body is distorted. At high altitudes, a person has to breathe heavily and randomly. Due to the low supply of oxygen, the victim also must experience an increased heart rate. All these factors contribute to the feelings of fear and worry. If a person has experienced a panic attack before, these symptoms may be too familiar and may lead to another panic attack right away. It is common for persons who have suffered from panic attacks to associated accelerated breathing and increased heart rate to panic attacks.

Generally, any person who fears or worries about something or the future will experience panic attacks. The things we worry about are not threatening. If you examine the reasons why you are afraid, you will realize that there is nothing alarming. If you suffer from anxiety or panic attacks, chances are that you have build up the fear within your mind. This leads us to the other cause of anxiety.

Internal causes of anxiety

The internal causes of anxiety are factors that are built within your mind. There is a close relationship between your mind, your emotions, and your behavior. If you show symptoms of anxiety, chances are that your mind has been corrupted by factors that you have allowed to grow internally. Some of the internal causes of anxiety include

Bitterness: Internal bitterness occurs when you choose to hold on to a situation that caused you pain. Bitterness is a state of emotion where an individual is constantly bitter due to events that occurred many years ago. Bitterness may stay within a person either consciously or subconsciously. If you harbor bitterness subconsciously, you may never know the causes of your anxiety. You will find yourself treating people around you as suspects, without knowing that your actions are informed by past life experiences.

Anger: Anger is another situation that may cause anxiety and panic attacks in a person. This is especially true if you let anger stay within your heart and mind for a long time. Through life circumstances, we all come to situations that may cause anger and bitterness. However, the way you deal with such a situation will determine whether you will live a free life or not. If you allow anger to stay within, it will eventually breed negativity, leading you to live a negative lifestyle. Living your life with a negative perspective will lead to anxiety and panic attacks. When you build up a negative perspective of life, you will never see any positive in any matter. You associate everyone and everything around you with negativity. This may be a dangerous place for anyone who wishes to live a happy life and enjoy love, success, and prosperity.

Fear: Fear is an emotional situation where an individual is constantly worried about the future or the past. The fact that you are worried about the future or the past is entrenched within your personality. Fear is mainly caused by past life experiences. The human brain creates an emotional association to past events. If you experience a positive event in your life, the brain will naturally associate such an event with positive emotions. If you experience a negative event or an event that caused negative emotions, you will naturally associate such an event with negativity. It is, therefore, important to ensure that you clear your mind of any events that may be associated with negativity. Negativity may mess up your normal thinking process and infiltrate your mind with fear or such like occurrences.

Beliefs and stereotypes: The human brain works in such a way that, whatever you feed it accepts it as the truth. When you tell your brain that something is bad and it believes it, it becomes impossible to overturn the situation. This is the reason why the world suffers from racism and tribalism. When most people are growing up, they are made to believe that a certain race or a certain tribe behaves in one way or another. Such beliefs are entrenched deep within a person, making that person a stone believer. Beliefs and stereotypes may lead to anxiety and panic attacks. If you believe that a certain person is dangerous based on their gender, race or tribe, you may experience fear in their presence.

Your intense fear and worry are not based on the fact that the said person is a threat, but it is based on the fact that you have allowed beliefs to take control of your mind. Allowing beliefs to take over can mess up the way you think and cause you to live in constant fear of the unknown.

Chapter 4
Understanding Anxiety

Anxiety is classified as an emotion; yet unlike love or joy, we tend to see it as something negative that is not supposed to be a part of our lives. However, since the earliest days that humans walked the earth, anxiety has served a purpose. It is a sensation that is intended to call us to alertness. It triggers the fight or flight reaction that has guided us for millennia in making our decisions when under stress. Yet, today, we tend to see it only as a negative and useless emotion. The question is why?

Despite us having changed the equatorial jungle for a concrete jungle, we are still in need of that early warning system that kept primitive humans safe. Anxiety can let us know when we don't feel comfortable in a situation or with a certain person. It can alert us to aspects of our psyche that require further development, and in small doses, it improves our mental functioning–allowing us to score better in tests and tasks that require heightened focus. Despite these valuable functions of anxiety, we want to stunt it today by medicating ourselves into fallaciously flavored bliss. What a loss this is to the human race, if we remove our ability to create awareness of our inner self and the world around us! For most of us, anxiety is that friend that we don't really want to play with, but they tag along with us, despite our best efforts to shoo them away. What if you turned back and decided to really look at anxiety, measure it up for its worth, its impact on your life, and begin to negotiate with it?

Unfortunately, some of us really struggle to face that uncertain playmate on our own, and when we lack the skills, and are not born with the talent to wrap up anxiety with a neat bow, we can succumb to depression and anxiety-related psychological disorders. When you don't know how to adequately address your anxieties, you could succumb to panic disorders, Post Traumatic Stress Disorder (PTSD), and other mental illnesses. When you feel unable to deal with your anxiety and your worries on your own, there is no shame in reaching out for professional help.

Why Do We Get Anxiety?

Psychologists will all tell you that anxiety is a normal emotion. It only becomes a problem when it goes into overdrive and begins reducing your abilities to cope with life. This can be best seen in extreme cases such as people who are so anxious about the world around them that they become reclusive and shut themselves off from society completely. For these people, the things that trigger their anxieties are simply more than they can face.

We can recognize the symptoms of anxiety quite easily. We have all, at some stage and to differing degrees, suffered the hyper-tension, pounding heart, raised blood pressure, and gnawing worries of anxiety that seem to dominate and destroy your life. If you continually suffer from anxiety in a certain setting or with certain people, you will likely begin to see these as triggers that set off the flood of anxiety. In turn, you will begin to fear those triggers and do everything in your power to avoid them. Sadly, this does not cure the anxiety, and you would be better served to start really looking at those triggers and what your anxiety is trying to tell you.

In the past, the triggers were situations or creatures that threatened us, and we had to decide whether we would fight off the predators, or if we would run from the stronger clan that moved onto our terrain. Today, the triggers may look different and instead of facing a saber-toothed tiger, we may be facing a vicious boss who dominates us or a relative that abuses us. Anxiety is the warning sign that something is going on, and it needs your attention (and decision-making skills) right now.

We commonly tend to say that we are stressed when we are actually feeling anxious, but whichever term you use, anxiety can have positive benefits to you in small and controlled amounts. The benefits can even outweigh the potential negatives of anxiety (Star, 2019).

- Self-Growth

Anxiety can help you learn about yourself. It can make you more aware of people, places, and situations that make you uncomfortable. We are often in denial about what we feel throughout our day, and if we keep avoiding an inconvenient truth about how we feel, anxiety tends to crop up to draw our attention back to that avoidance. Next time you feel anxious about someone, take the time to ask yourself why. You may have been conditioned to be polite to someone when actually there is something about them that sets your warning bells ringing. Feeling anxious may be a result of loads of tiny stimuli that you have not even consciously been aware of noticing. You may find a certain look that someone gives you to be disturbing, yet you try and avoid thinking of this observation since it goes against how you are preconditioned to treat that person. Unease, disquiet, and suspicions are all derivatives of anxiety that help you evaluate whether people can be trusted or not.

- Motivator

You can use the energy of anxiety to become more motivated. Like the early humans were able to get that extra boost of energy to run away from predators, you can use the energy to increase your mental awareness, physical alertness, and thinking skills. However, if you let anxiety overwhelm you, it will lead to draining your motivation and can trigger depression. That energy has to go somewhere, so it's better that you channel it constructively. In a mentally trying situation such as writing a test, a small amount of anxiety helps you focus and recall all that you have learned. However, in a social setting such as going on a date, the energy may present as being nervous and could end up costing you a pleasant evening. In this case, you would need to channel that energy into a positive direction such as a mindfulness task, a distraction, or even physical movement. This is why dancing is such a great icebreaker for those who are prone to feeling a little anxious.

- Safety

Healthy amounts of anxiety keep us alert to potential dangers in life. It is what makes us look before crossing a road, and it helps us to avoid situations that could cause us harm. Being utterly fearless would lead us into situations and places where we will likely be injured and seriously harmed. In this sense, small amounts of anxiety are equivalent to common sense. It helps us realize that something is dangerous before we are hurt.

- Fosters Empathy

If you know anxiety, and you have learned to look it in the face, you will have developed a much treasured and often rare skill–empathy. You will understand that people are not always feeling up to a challenge, and that it's okay to be scared. Instead of telling people (and yourself) to suck it up, you will be able to help them (and yourself) live peaceful and self-embracing lives.

- Makes for Good Leaders

Healthy amounts of anxiety can lead to being cautious, considering what happens, and what could happen. This stimulates effective planning and responsible decision making. In excessive amounts, anxiety can make leaders act obsessively and take decisions based on unrealistic fears, though many highly passionate leaders throughout history have displayed the traits of anxiety, which might explain some controversial decisions that they made.

Anxiety may have many positives to those who are able to tame their inner fears and develop the skills to conquer and use it. However, if you do not learn how to manage your anxiety, you will fall subject to its whims, and like a fickle ruler, it can ruin your life.

You Are Not Alone

One of the biggest challenges to you if you suffer from anxiety is that you probably believe you are the only one who is dealing with those nagging worries, negative thoughts, cold sweats, sleep deprivation, numbness, nausea, and a whole list of other embarrassing and painful symptoms. You probably feel like a massive failure and a loser. News flash–you are not alone.

Since anxiety is a normal emotion, we all "suffer" from it from time to time. Suffering from anxiety is, however, your choice. You can choose to think of it as the enemy; or you can accept that it is normal, we all have it, and you can learn to control and use it. It may be painful to initially make that mind shift but once you do, it will vastly improve your approach to life, and the way in which you think about your fears.

In the digital age that we live in with information at our fingertips, we are constantly surrounded by fear-inspiring news, overwhelming and often fake standards that are promulgated on social media, and the pressure of staying connected and online. The fear of missing out (FOMO) can be hugely detrimental to our existence, and we become anxious when we're not able to be online or participate in Internet-driven activities. Oddly, in being "connected" in the age of technology, we have become very disconnected from ourselves. In knowing yourself, making peace with your feelings, and accepting your needs, as well as meeting them holistically, you can overcome the fear-driven behaviors of anxiety.

Chapter 5

What is Buddhism?

Buddhism is more popular today than it was half a century ago. Many people have realized that they would like to pursue this way of life, especially because of the amazing benefits it provides for the mind and body. When you decide to pursue Buddhism, your main goal is to obtain a state of lasting, unconditional happiness known as enlightenment. Every Buddhists goal is to reach enlightenment and to be able to reach this, you must use practical tools like meditation to gain your insight and develop compassion and wisdom. Every single person is able to tap into their potential and realize that the ultimate goal is enlightenment.

Buddhism is a way of life that will lead to the discernment of what true reality is. Its focus is to help you develop the ability to be mindful and be aware of your actions, thoughts, and surroundings. All of these will initially lead to a life that is fully in tune with nature and your true self within. It may be hard to get a grasp on at first, but everything that happens in your life is dictated by your thoughts and emotions and when you meditate, you will get a clearer look at what needs to change in your world, as well as discovering more about who is in relation to the bigger picture that you are apart of and the world that you live in, as well as the body that you inhabit.

One of the most important teachings in Buddhism is the understanding that where you are in this exact moment is exactly where you are supposed to be. As every event comes and time passes, you are following your own course throughout life and enjoying everything that comes to you. Each moment plays an important part in creating a path of wisdom and understanding just for yourself. Take in each and every sentence and take the time to fully understand what you are doing. Every teaching can pave the way to a more joyful, enlightened, and open path in your life.

Buddhism is actually not a religion technically, at least not in the sense that there is an institution that dictates how somebody should believe in specific higher power. Many people make the mistake of believing that Buddhism has that characteristic and they end up avoiding it because they don't want it to be contrary to the teachings they experience in a church. But you can, in fact, practice Buddhism at the same time as your personal beliefs and/or religion, and it will only compliment it.

In Buddhism, there isn't a god to be worshipped, although there are worshipping statues called Buddhas, Buddhist just pay respect to the memory of the Buddha. It always helps as a guide to what you are doing. Buddha is neither worshipped nor prayed, too. He is simply a guide and teacher for those that seek the initial path to enlightenment. The altars you may see while exploring Buddhism are simply an inspiration and are there to remind people to practice the path they have chosen to walk.

Many people that wake up in the morning intending to practice Buddhist teachings often find inspiration from the image of Buddha. It is not like finding your motivation from the words of a successful figure. His peaceful and meditative image can help you understand the teaching you are following when life becomes stressful and your mind begins to run off course.

The main practices of Buddhism include yoga and meditation. They are meant to help you unlearn and break away from your past preconceived notions of yourself and the world. They will serve as your guide towards fully embracing qualities like love, wisdom, kindness, and awareness. Over the course of your youth, you are taught the values of your society and they may not be in tune with true values which is why the reminder is needed. Look at all of the uncertainty that resides in the world, and at the bottom of it all, you will always a find a line of thought that leads you to the unhappiness that you experience in your life.

Those who continue to participate in the path of Buddhism often find themselves achieving the state of enlightenment. In other words, they become a Buddha. A Buddha is simply being someone who has been able to see the nature of life for what it truly is. An enlightened being will then continue to live life fully, all while holding onto the principles that are in line with this specific vision. Since your philosophy of Buddhism may question your current values, you need to stay open-minded enough to learn the teachings because they are very direct. To reach the ultimate goal of enlightenment, you will need to let go of the values that may, at the current time, be essential to who you are.

In other belief systems, these are given names, often known as the soul. Although you can give it any name, it is important what you decide to name it for yourself. It is important that you recognize that these two parts of you exist. If you are unhappy in your life, your balance and harmony are essentially missing and that is where Buddhism can help you align your values so that both parts of you are in harmony with each other.

Every human being has the opportunity to become enlightened in whatever life they decide to live, there is no set course for your life. Karma plays a major part in deciding the circumstances of your life, especially in which you will be born from life to life. Your own spiritual and mental ambition and how you embrace it is what drives each person to take the step closer to enlightenment. When you follow the path of Buddhism, you do not have one big goal for the end. It is a paradox for someone to declare they are using Buddhism just to reach enlightenment.

Chapter 6

Who is Buddha?

The word "Buddha" translates back to "enlightened one" or "awakened being." It refers to any person that has reached this state, however, here are some things you may want to know about the real Buddha.

According to ancient legend, the first Buddha was named Siddhartha Gautama. Most people believe that he was born in the B.C. time era, in a land that is now found in Nepal. It is said that the Buddha was born a royal and shielded from the suffering of the kingdom that his father build, a grand palace that was full of religion and suffering. Buddha had an entire world created within that walls of the castle, and as Buddha grew, he was led to believe that the world outside was one made of empathy, joy, and happiness. The king was told by fortune tellers that when his son was born, he would be a great spiritual leader and a warrior.

Later in Buddha's life, after he was raised and has been married, he ventured out into the real world and saw everything that his father had been hiding from him. He saw the truth of humanity and met an old man, which he then gained the knowledge that all people age and eventually die. After figuring all of this out, he then decided he wanted to go out into the world and explore as many religions across the world as he could to find the answer to the questions we would all ask ourselves such as "where do we find happiness?" He tried many ways including fasting and when he found that fasting was irrelevant, he decided to meditate on the problems he faced. While others still decided to fast, he decided to go about finding another route, one that would lead to enlightenment.

Several years into his spiritual adventure, Buddha encountered something called "The Middle Path" while meditating under a tree. This path was a way of balance without using extreme measures which he found only through many trials and much error. Buddha sat under the tree for days seeking the answers he had set out for. During this meditation, Buddha had to face a demon known as Mara who had threatened to stand in the way of his Buddha status. He looked to mother earth for answers and the land answered by banishing Mara and allowing Buddha to reach complete enlightenment. After this life-changing experience, while meditating, Buddha lived the rest of his life trying to inform and share with everything that he had discovered. People began to follow his ways and eventually named his principle the Dharma, which translates back to "Truth."

When you hear the word suffering, you instantly think of pain and anger, but in Buddhism, they believe that all of life is suffering. As humans, we feel the pain of life which includes loss, happiness, sadness, disappointment, and so on. These emotions are manifestations of our mind, and they don't come from our inner self. Because they do not come from one's inner self, they are depicted as suffering. These are initially false feelings that were created by our brains and programmed into us by what our society has taught us. The way forward was believed to be the Noble Eightfold Path and this allowed people to get closer to reaching enlightenment.

In this day and age, Buddhism is increasingly becoming a popular way of life for millions of people all around the world. People generally like the concept of Buddhism just because what they find speaks to their heart and that is how it should be. Regardless of what your views and values are if Buddhism speaks to you, it is encouraged that you explore the teachings and try to pursue it, but only if you want to and if you feel it is right for you. Scientists and researchers have explored the relationship between the Buddhist teachings and the way that the brain operates, they found that Buddhist monks were able to use the creative side of their brain and the calculating side of their brain at the time, therefore, more open to creativity.

In a world where everything is in constant motion, always forcing us to move forward at a quicker and more rapid pace, many people lose their connection with nature and the connection with themselves. Though nature is all around us, what we have done as human beings to change the pure form of the earth creates a disconnection from our minds. In Buddhism, you are reminded to be constantly connected with every natural thing in the world, and by practicing the teachings of Buddhism, you are brought back to a connection with the earth. Think of it as connecting back to your original roots.

If you are unsure of what this means, you only have to go back to nature to get inspired. The feelings you experience don't just come from your external stimuli. They come from your inner self recognizing the joy that lies in the ever-moving thing called nature. Go up to the mountains and ground yourself with the beauty this world beholds. Another reason why Buddhism is so widespread around the world is the fact that the Buddha never claimed to be a god. Instead, he wanted to be seen as a teacher and somebody that helped others with his wisdom based on his own experiences in life.

Buddhism can be found in every natural effect on mother earth, from the worms in the soil to the leaves on the trees. They are the story of the past, but you don't need to look to the past to find enlightenment. To find enlightenment, you have to look at all of the moments that you experience. Buddhists never seek to convince others of a certain belief. Instead, they only provide an explanation of it if they are asked. Buddha encourages one to be curious through awareness, therefore, Buddhism can be seen more as a way of life that is based on discernment rather than faith like most are.

Mindfulness forms a very important part of the philosophy of Buddhism. You are losing the opportunity to enjoy when you are not present at that moment that you are in. Regardless of how many problems you encounter in life, being mindful can help you to overcome any obstacles that are placed in your way and to get beyond those problems in healthy ways.

Buddhism is an awareness of self, awareness of your surroundings, and awareness of others. Without this awareness, you lose out on a lot of benefits. By having awareness, you are able to empathize with others and encourage them to do the same. You are also then able to control the way that you interact with others and keep your negativity to a bare minimum. Whether you decide to realize it or not, all of your unhappiness stems from you. Although you may feel the need to blame others for any negative feelings you are experiencing. Buddhism helps you to understand this impact and to work on lessening the impact it has on you.

Chapter 7
The Teachings of Buddhism

The Way of Investigation

The very first teaching of Buddha is to investigate everything and not accept anything that is based on blind faith. He advised people to discover the truth of everything and anything that they encounter. He pointed out that most of the problems were induced by believing in things that are not based on tradition. The right way to accept things is to have an open mind and dig a little deeper into the development, origin, and characteristics of things, just so that you know the whole truth about everything. Similarly, he said that people should only explore Buddhism after investigating meditation and thinking about Buddhism while using meditation.

Four Noble Truths

During the course of Buddha's life, especially while working towards reaching enlightenment, Buddha discovered the four noble truths. These are the truths you need to accept and understand if you want to reach complete happiness and peace in your life.

The first truth of Buddhism is the 'Truth of Dukkha', which states that each of us is affected by some sort of suffering in this world. There are two types of suffering: physical and mental. Mental problems are the emotional disturbances we experience after going through a traumatic experience or difficult time in life and physical suffering refers to the physical harm, pain, and injury we experience.

The second truth in Buddhism is 'the truth regarding the creation of dukkha'. This truth explains that the main cause of suffering is your ignorance and desires. Ignorance is not being conscious of the reality of things and just completely living a life of delusion. Desires refer to all of your wants that make you indulge in practices that bring different kinds of harm and pain to your life.

The third truth in Buddhism is 'the truth pertinent to the ending of all suffering'. This truth states that by working on eliminating all of the things in your life that are negative or bring negativity from your mind and life, you can rid your life of all sufferings and reach the state of complete peace, serenity, and happiness.

The fourth truth to Buddhism is 'the truth of following the middle way that ends all dukkha'. This truth is said to contain complete peace and happiness. You need to follow the middle way, also known as the eightfold noble path. By following this path, you can live a more balanced life, which is neither careless nor too difficult. It is just perfect and helps you live a perfectly happy and beautiful life.

Eightfold path

The eightfold noble path is known as the middle way that sets out the guidelines you need to follow to deal with every type of hardships and sufferings. This way of life compromised of eight rules that you follow when you are following Buddhism.

Samma ditthi or right view/understanding: You need to reevaluate your understanding of things and view things the right way so that you can gain complete insight into them. This means correcting your view of this life and not getting attracted to the worldly pleasures and desires because when this happens, you become very involved in this world and strive just to obtain those pleasures that will eventually result in suffering. Try to mentally understand what you really desire in your life that will ultimately bring you the absolute happiness in your life and not just temporary happiness that is brought to you by the worldly possessions and desires. Secondly, you need to understand that you inflict suffering on yourself with or without knowing it, so end it and correct your vision of things.

Samma Sankappa or Right Thought: Next, you need to focus on correcting your thought process, which can be accomplished if you correct your intention. For that, you need to reject the pleasures the world tries to dangle in front of you and instead bring love, kindness, and compassion for others in your thoughts.

Samma Vacca or Right Speech: You need to work on correcting your speech and the way you speak to people, which can be done if you practice abstinence from bad grammar, gossip, cruel speech, arguing, and idle chitchatting.

Samma Kammanta or Right Action: You must improve your actions and correct them by giving yourself a cleansing and ridding yourself of all sorts of sexual misconducts, destructive, and illegal actions.

Samma Ajiva or Right Livelihood: You need to work on the way that you make a living and must not do anything that will harm any other living being. Buddha instructed that you absolutely cannot practice these five professions: dealing in ammunition and arms, dealing in the flesh (butcher), dealing in sex and human trafficking, dealing in any sort of drugs, and dealing in any poisonous substances.

Samma Vayama or Right Effort: You need to correct your efforts. For that, you need to think in the right direction which may be a different direction. The sixth, seventh, and eighth factors are interlinked and closely related.

Samma Satti or Right Mindfulness: You need to work on reaching the state of mindfulness, which means you need to be aware of everything that is happening inside you and around you. This can be reached by practicing the eighth factor.

Samma Samadhi or Right Concentration: Lastly, you need to work on your concentration and focus. You must be fully concentrated on a subject to be aware of it and to understand it better. Right effort, concentration, and mindfulness can only be reached with meditation; hence, meditation is a very important tool of Buddhism.

By following these eight factors, you can live a more balanced, smooth, and composed life that is free of all sufferings.

Karma

Karma refers to actions that humans make and the law of action. It states that every single action has a reaction. If you do bad things, bad things consume your speech, body, and mind and harm you, then you will get painful results that you may not like. If you are living a life full of hardships, then it is a reflection of the bad things you chose to do.

Rebirth

Buddha believed in rebirth. He states that the reason why some people are born rich or poor is because of the good or bad things they did in their lives. According to Buddha, a person is born many times and rebirth goes far beyond the human realm and into the spiritual realm. He believed that people could be born as an animal, a bird, or even a spirit. The different realms that exist within are the human realm, grim and lower realms, ghost realm, animal and bird realm, and heavenly realm. Human beings can come or go into any of those realms if they desire.

Chapter 8

The Four Noble Truths

When Buddha started teaching about his enlightenment, he started with the Four Noble Truths. In these truths, Buddha is teaching about suffering, its cause, how there is an end to suffering, and what to do so you can end suffering.

Dukkha

Dukkha is the truth that states that suffering exists. Dukkha is real and universal, and there are several causes of suffering. Some of these causes are sickness, the impermanence of pleasure, and pain. Dukkha states that our suffering often starts because we have a desire that we can't fulfill.

No matter what we want, we continue to suffer because when we reach one goal, we want more. This is human nature, and Buddhists feel that in order to fully reach the path of enlightenment, we need to understand dukkha and take control of it so that we can control our suffering and take the next step toward entering the pure state of mind. An example of this is money. How often do we state that if we just had more money, we could buy a nicer car or a bigger house? However, once we attain this level of wealth, we still want more money because we want more things.

Samudaya

Samudaya states that there is a cause for suffering, which is the desire to control things. Some people refer to this as the cravings or thirst for things that we can't have at the moment. There can be many forms of samudaya, such as the desire for fame, craving of sexual pleasures, and the desire to avoid unpleasant sensations, such as anger, jealousy, and fear. Buddhists also state that this craving creates karma, which is what makes you want more. When we suffer, we are ignoring karma because we are too worried about our own selfish desires and wishes.

When we let suffering take over, it's because we've let go of what really matters and started to focus on our wants. For instance, we start looking toward our neighbors to see what they have in life, and we begin to want that. We want the bigger car, the bigger house, and nicer clothes. We work on trying to impress others instead of focusing on compassion, understanding, keeping our minds clear, and karma. We also start blaming others for our own problems instead of looking inside ourselves to see if we can find an answer and cure for our problems.

In the eyes of Buddha, anything that made you unhappy or took away your peace was a cause of suffering. When the word suffering came to Buddha, it didn't just have to do with seeing people become sick, die, or get physically hurt. It also had to do with allowing ourselves to become unhappy, clouding our minds with unwelcome thoughts, such as "I have this, but it's not good enough, so now I want this."

Nirodha

Nirodha gives us the realization that there is an end to suffering, and this comes when we finally reach the liberation of nirvana. In Buddhism, the only true way to end suffering is to end your wants and wishes and your selfish desires. You need to become free of those thoughts. In order to do this, you need to understand the right view from the Eightfold Path. Only then will you be able to realize that suffering can end if we let go of what we want and find happiness within ourselves. Once this is attained, we let go of all the cravings we have and are truly free of our suffering.

Megga

Megga is the fourth Noble Truth, which states that the only way we can work toward ending our suffering is by following the Eightfold Path, or the Middle Path. To end suffering, you need to follow a path. One of the best ways to understand this path of ending suffering, along with the Four Noble Truths, is to look at this as if you had an illness. For example, dukka is the diagnosis. This is the part where the doctor tells you what illness you have, and you come to realize that you have this illness. The next step of the process is finding the cause. What caused this illness? In other words, what caused this suffering that you've realized is inside of you? The third step, which is nirodha, is the treatment phase of the process. Now that you have observed you're suffering and you've found the cause, you can come up with a plan to help treat the suffering. The final phase, which is megga, is the recovery phase. This is the part where you've been able to get through the suffering and you're liberated.

Of course, it's important to realize and remember that no matter how hard we try, we can't get rid of suffering in the world. It's just part of life, and we need to learn to deal with it and, at times, overcome it. We suffer when we are born; we just have no remembrance of it. We also suffer when we are growing up and growing old. We also suffer because of death and other situations that happen in our lives, such as heartaches. Buddhism isn't about getting rid of suffering or finding ways, so you don't have to feel like you are suffering; it's more about working to ease the suffering. Buddhism can work to try to give you an understanding of your suffering and why suffering exists in this world.

Chapter 9

Karma, Nirvana, Reincarnation

Karma

As indicated by the British savant Alan Watts, Karma in Buddhist and Hindu way of thinking shows "The related origin of the considerable number of structures and periods of life." You can't just credit an Eastern way of thinking to a Western perspective without having a nearby take a gander at its cause. You need to think about that Karma is a piece of a greater roundabout, profound picture. It includes rebirth and realizing that everything is associated. Western thought doesn't give space for us to imagine that we are the texture of the universe. Be that as it may, we are.

Buddhism instructs us that we are not minor, unimportant bits on a desolate little planet. We are, in certainty, a piece of everything around us, and everything that happens is occurring as it should. It isn't dependent upon us to control our general surroundings. We need to control what is inside ourselves, and this way, we become some portion of everything.

Karma includes the possibility of congruity with a pattern. Individuals search for designs all over the place. It is a piece of our characteristic make-up and a central explanation behind the endurance of our species. At the point when history rehashes itself, it will, in general, do as such with great karma or terrible karma. Karma rises above numerous cycles of life, so you won't receive the rewards of what you sow in this lifetime.

Karma isn't a momentary reward framework. It is a lot of qualities that are intended to encourage all of us to improve. The greater individuals do, the greater will happen to it. You shouldn't be in it for yourself, yet for the development of more noteworthy benefits. The individuals on the planet will continue evolving. They will travel every which way. Be that as it may, the more individuals cling to the lessons of karma, the better the world will become for everybody.

Consider a war that has been continuing for a considerable length of time or hundreds of years. The individuals battling the war today are not the individuals who began the war. On the off chance that you think negative musings and perform damaging activities, the karmic cycle of antagonism and decimation will proceed. Individuals need to settle on a cognizant choice to change dangerous examples of conduct. They have to spread cherishing consideration and sincere goals to break the unlimited cycles of war. It requires more significant levels of reasoning and comparable profound qualities. Everybody needs to make an individual commitment to achieve the undertaking of realizing harmony known to humanity.

Karma directs; in case you plant an oak seed, an oak will develop. The oak will deliver oak seeds, and the cycle of development will proceed.

In the event that you plant a spoiled seed, nothing will develop. That is karma.

Karma as activity and response: if we show goodness, we will procure goodness.

Karma is the all-inclusive standard of circumstances and logical results. Our activities, both great and awful, return to us later on, helping us to gain from life's exercises and become better individuals. In religions that incorporate resurrection, karma reaches out through one's present life and all past and future lives also.

Karma, in itself, is basic energy. One individual tosses out energy through considerations, words, and activities, and it returns, in time, through other individuals. Karma is the best educator, compelling individuals to confront the outcomes of their behavior and along these lines improve and refine their conduct or endure in the event that they don't. Indeed, even brutal karma, when looked in insight, can be the best flash for profound development. The triumph of karma lies in clever activity and dispassionate reaction.

Supporting any activity, with the case, "I am doing it," is karma. Affirming any activity ties karma, and then, the binding karma supports the action with the conviction 'I am the practitioner.' In the event that you realize that you are not the practitioner and know about who the genuine practitioner is, 'I am not the practitioner' and 'who is the practitioner' at that point, the activity won't have any help, and the karma will be shed.

Nirvana

The term Nirvana in Buddhism is mostly used to show the definitive spiritual objective of accomplishing a condition of enlightenment which discharges one from the cycle of rebirth. The term alludes to the dousing of three flames inside oneself, every one of which speaks to ravenousness, disdain, and daydream, with the goal that one can arrive settled and profound satisfaction. Present-day elucidations recommend a "nirvana in this life" is conceivable reliant on a changed condition of the character described by empathy, harmony, profound otherworldly delight, and a nonappearance of negative mental states and feelings, for example, question, stress, tension, and dread.

Reincarnation

According to the Buddha, we all will pass away in the end in the regular procedure of birth, mature age, and demise and that we ought to consistently remember the fleetingness of life: The existence that we as a whole appreciate and wish to hang on to.

To Buddhism, death isn't the end of life, it is simply the termination of our body in this world, yet our soul will, in any case, remain and search out through the need of connection, connection to another body, and new life. Where they will be conceived is an aftereffect of the past and the amassing of positive and negative activity, and the resultant karma (circumstances and logical results) is a consequence of one's past activities.

This would prompt the individual to be re-awakened in one of 6 domains, which are; paradise, people, Asura, hungry apparition, creature, and hellfire. Domains, as per the seriousness of one's karmic activities, Buddhists accept in any case, none of these spots are perpetual, and one doesn't stay in wherever uncertainly. Therefore, in Buddhism, life doesn't end; it simply goes on in different structures that are the aftereffect of gathered karma. Buddhism is a conviction that underlines the temporariness of lives, including every one of those past the present life. In light of this, we ought not to fear to pass as it will prompt resurrection.

The dread of death originated from the dread of the stop to be existent and losing one's personality and a dependable balance on the planet. We see our passing coming sometime before its appearance, and we see fleetingness in the progressions we see about us and to us in the appearance of maturing and the enduring due to losing our childhood. When we were solid and lovely and as we age, as we approach our last snapshots of life, we understand how short-lived such an agreeable spot really was.

The idea of resurrection or rebirth has gotten increasingly prominent in the west as of late because of the impact of Tibetan Buddhism. Normally individuals worry about life past death was animated by the thoughts contained in such methods of reasoning and convictions.

The incomparable point of Buddhism is to acquire nirvana or illumination. This shows a condition of freedom or brightening from the impediments of presence. It is the freedom from the push of resurrection through incalculable lives here, and there the six realities. It is gotten through the termination of want.

Nirvana is an express that is realistic in this life through the correct yearning, immaculateness of life, and the disposal of narcissism. This discontinuance of presence as we probably are aware of it, the achievement of being, as particular from turning out to be. The Buddha discusses it as unborn, un-began, uncreated, unformed, standing out it from the conceived, started, made, and shaped the extraordinary world. The individuals who have acquired the province of Nirvana are called Buddhas. Gautama Siddhartha had acquired this state and had become a Buddha at 35. Anyway, it is currently accepted that it was simply after he had passed away that he arrived at such a position of immaculate serenity since some buildup of human pollution would keep on existing as long as his physical body existed.

Chapter 10
Uncovering the Secret of Zen

What Is Zen Meditation?

Zen Meditation is an outgrowth of Buddhism. Zen is primarily a Japanese development of Buddhism, but it does not have to be linked to that religion and can be practiced by anyone, anywhere. The word Zen is derived from "Chan," a Chinese school of Buddhism or possibly from the word dhyana, which simply means meditation. Whole books have been written tracing the development and etymology of the word "Zen," but you don't actually have to know any of that in order to be able to practice Zen meditation. Later on, you might want to read some of the extensive literature that is associated with Zen and with Buddhism as inspiration, but for right now our concern is simply what is meditation and how to do it.

Meditation can actually be a lot of different things. It can be a focused practice of mindfulness while doing repetitive manual tasks, such as shelling peas, washing dishes, digging ditches or mopping floors. It can be concentration on a candle flame, mandala or repeated syllables that are spoken out loud. It can be meditation-in-motion, such as is practiced by martial artists who learn a set of movements called forms or a set of asanas such as might be practiced in Yoga. But Zen takes meditation down to its very simplest and sometimes most difficult form: sitting meditation.

Sitting meditation is difficult because it does not give the body any way to distract and occupy the physical system while the mind is meditating. It is not sleep or daydreaming—although both of those things have been known to occur during meditation times. Those who have attended a Meeting of the Society of Friends of Jesus (otherwise known as Quakers) might have observed those times when some of the Elders in the meeting dose off while observing silence. Polite members of the Meeting will ignore the sonorous snores that sometimes punctuate such a gathering.

Sitting meditation can be exceptionally difficult for those who are accustomed to nearly constant movement, such as those whose work is physically active or demanding. It is equally difficult for the Millennium generation because they must unplug themselves, as it were, and cease data input for a span of time. But sitting meditation, or zazen, is the heart of Zen.

Sitting meditation has several steps, and it can be part of a more elaborate system of exercises such as yoga, ordinary exercise workouts or as the beginning or closing of a day. But it can also provide a time-out during a busy day that provides clarity and stills the busy mind that can become a distraction. These are actually simple steps and do not require elaborate preparation or extreme dedication. One follower Chinese disciple of a follower of Buddha is said to have sat zazen so long that his legs fell off, and he is said to have later cut off his eyelids to keep from falling asleep.

Frankly, as a modern person who practices meditation, this writer classes these stories in the same category as the Paul Bunyan or Davie Crockett legends of the American west. Such tall tales are supreme exaggerations of real situations. Perhaps the original person sat so long that his legs fell asleep—not unusual once one is used to meditation; or perhaps he had a habit of going to sleep while supposedly meditating. Or, more likely, these were cautionary stories told to young monks by older ones who wanted appropriate action by the youngsters without extreme behavior.

One method to avoid sitting in meditation for an overly long amount of time or to gauge whether one has sat long enough is to invest in a timer that has a soft, bell-like chime. The regular kitchen timer with the annoying buzzer will keep track of time just as well, but the harsh sound can jangle nerves and partially defeat the serenity you might hope to achieve through meditation.

Let's face it: humans are not naturally serene. They are an argumentative, competitive, emotional lot that are more prone to rationalize than to think rationally. Meditation won't cure all of that, but it can help the practitioner hew out a space in his or her day to let the brain cells stop being busy with the tumbling thoughts that live in each of us. Once the chattering monkey mind is stilled, then inspiration, solutions to problems or just a wonderful sense of peace can rise to the surface. Deeper in, even those things are stilled, and the self-perception stops, merging into a perception of Self as part of everything, and then simply perception of the Deep Stillness. Out of that stillness comes real Inspiration, the life-changing revelations—or not. Sometimes all that comes of it is a sense of peace, which can in and of itself be life changing.

Unless you are a very exceptional person, you won't get there the first time you try meditation; you might not even get there the fiftieth time. Leo Babauto, author of Zen Habits, writes that most people do not understand the art of doing nothing. While meditation isn't actually doing nothing—it is doing something—getting past the need to Do Something is one part of learning to meditate.

Robert Anson Heinlein, in his science fiction novel Glory Road wrote that Americans are a busy people. He went on to say that a Frenchman could easily sit at a café and wait, while the empty coffee cups piled up around him, but that the American culture is one that encourages industry-in-motion.

Perhaps that is why the early Zen movement in the United States overlapped with the drug counterculture. The whole idea of simply sitting down, sitting still and doing nothing was foreign to the mainstream American mind in the 1950s and 1960s. The 1970s showed a little promise, coming out of the consciousness raising sessions and communal experiments of the 60s, but the falling economy of the 1980s and continued budget crunch of the 90s through many people back into the "keep moving, make some money, survive" mode of living and thinking.

But no historical event is without the ability to teach; and no decade is without its gems of wisdom that can be passed on to the next generation of learners and thinkers. Zen entered Japan sometime around the 7th Century CE (Common Era) but did not fully develop until around the 12th Century. This was about the time of the ending of the Pax Romana in Europe and around the Mediterranean, and the beginning of what is sometimes referred to as the Dark Ages. In actual fact, the Pax Romana sort of whimpered its way out over time and never quite totally died, and the Dark Ages were actually a time when a number of new ideas and concepts emerged—but that is quite a different story, although one that is interesting. I digress.

Back to the topic at hand: Zen Meditation. Not all Zen masters fully agree on what constitutes Zen meditation, so it is no wonder that other people are a bit confused by it. The truth is that the practice is highly individual, although learning how to do it is facilitated by the presence of an experienced teacher. While there are a number of YouTube videos available currently that purport to instruct in the art of meditation (and some of them are not bad), there is no experience that is quite like being face-to-face with an experienced Zen meditation instructor. Which is not to say that one cannot learn to meditate without an instructor; but instruction can keep the new practitioner from chasing red herrings down mental rabbit holes, as it were.

For example, out in central Missouri in 1962 there were not a lot of Zen instructors available for a twelve-year-old girl who wanted to explore the concept. In fact, she fell into the practice quite by accident thanks to having ordered an illustrated book about Yoga. Yoga is made for the twelve-year-old body, which is still flexible enough to turn into a pretzel without days or even weeks of steady practice to stretch joints—although a spotter would have been nice when she was learning headstands.

Part of that Yoga book was devoted to meditation—sitting, standing, and lying down—meditation was something that a farm girl who spent a lot of time alone could easily do on those lazy afternoons when all of the adults were taking a siesta.

Now, let's fast forward that young woman about six years to her first year in college. She went to a Midwestern United States college that provided the opportunity for students to earn their tuition by working four hours every day. The girl's first job was in the college's candy kitchen—a hot, sticky place to work during the summer. One afternoon, the power went out and the supervisor and her crew were left sitting in an overly warm sub-basement while waiting for the air conditioning, lights and power to the stoves to come back on. The girl knew that one way to handily pass time and to block out physical discomfort was to pass that time in meditation. What she had not counted on was the panic her stillness and ability to ignore her surroundings would create in those who were not experienced in meditation. The supervisor actually shook her by the shoulder to bring her back up from deep meditation. This left her disorientated for several minutes, while she brought the real world back into focus.

Needless to say, this was a lesson learned. She never, after that, meditated in an area where there were inexperienced people about who would not understand that a person who is meditating needs to be brought back up to the real world gently. It is probable that the supervisor suspected that she had taken some sort of drug the year was 1970, after all but the girl had taken nothing. Having had eight years of sporadic, but frequent sessions of study and practice, she was very good at meditation. It should be noted here that for the beginner, sitting too long in meditation is far less of a problem than being able to judge how long one has been meditating. Humans just are not geared toward doing nothing. Really, they aren't—especially not these days. They are in the habit of always doing something—texting, playing video games, watching television, working, playing face-to-face games, talking, even exercising. Sitting down to meditate just might be one of the hardest things that a busy person can do. Setting a timer for the amount of time to be spent in actual meditation helps diminish the habit of meditating with one eye on the clock to see how many more minutes one is supposed to be continuing the activity. Clock watching is a distraction that no beginning meditator needs. In fact, one suspects that clock watching was one of the functions of a meditation teacher—although there are certainly others. For directions for how to get started with Zen Meditation if you do not have a teacher and anticipate having to practice alone for some time to come. That still, small place that is so huge when you get there is available to everyone, and does not require special equipment, special instruction or special anything. It is yours; now, let us go look for the path to find it.

Chapter 11 Preparing for meditation

While meditation can be undertaken virtually anywhere, at any time, there are certain guidelines to follow if you want your meditation to be as effective as possible. However, keep in mind that meditation is meant to be flexible. The idea is not to create a rigid system that you will have a hard time following. Meditation aims to be easy and adaptable to suit your specific needs.

Sitting And Posture

We start by discussing the five basic meditative postures. Your job is to determine which attitude works for you in most situations and stick to it. Although you have to follow a specific meditative posture for certain meditative exercises, most can also be adapted to alternative postures.

Chair Meditation

Since most of us tend to have 9-to-5 jobs, we realistically tend to sit in some office chair for most of our time. Chair meditation is a great way to break through your afternoon monotony without ever having to leave your station. For seated meditation, you want to straighten your back and make sure you hit the floor with your feet. Ideally, your knees should be bent at a 90-degree angle and your back should be as straight as possible. If you're not sure what to do with your hands, just rest them on your knees.

Standing Meditation

Sometimes you want to get out of your chair and it may be more pleasant to try a standing method. You will want to start standing so that your feet are shoulder-length apart. Bend your knees slightly and relieve pressure throughout your day down to your feet. As you do this, adjust your hands so that they are gently placed over your abdomen so that you can feel every breath moving through your body as you embark on your personal mission.

Cross-Legged Meditation

Another pose that you can explore if you feel comfortable is the traditional Indian cross-legged. This particular posture is actually the most recommended posture of meditative activities, the idea being to keep your legs crossed, hips slightly higher than the heels of your feet. If you are new to meditation, it is generally recommended to try this pose with a pillow or towel or some kind of soft surface underneath so that you don't hurt yourself as it can be difficult to hold when that are not used to it. If you feel there is too much pressure on your heels, try bringing one of your legs over the other so that the ankle is one above the knee of the other leg. You can also bring full heels over the thighs of the other leg in what is commonly known as the Lotus position.

The Burmese pose is slightly different because you don't cross your legs. Instead, you can position your feet so that the ankles of each foot are bent inward and facing the pubic area - this pose is generally preferred by people who have a hard time crossing their legs.

Kneeling Meditation

If you want to keep your back straight but don't feel comfortable crossing your legs, another great alternative is kneeling. Traditionally this is known as the Virasana or the Vajrasana. Here you start by bending your knees and resting your body weight along the length of your shins. Your ankles should be tucked under your buttocks. For convenience and comfort, you can choose to place a rolled-up yoga mattress or some type of tube between your buttocks and your knees.

This particular position is usually easier than sitting cross-legged and is also generally pain-free, so your ankles will thank you.

Horizontal Meditation

However, if none of these positions suit you, or if you try a sleep-inducing meditation, you will find that the chosen posture is generally the horizontal posture. When laying down, make sure that your feet are shoulder-length, similar to the standing meditation position, and that your arms are at your sides instead of being folded over your body. If you find this position uncomfortable, you can bend your knees and lift your hips slightly to help yourself adjust.

Tuning Into Physical Sensations

The physical world around you affects your mind. This is a fact we all know. What we don't necessarily notice is that just as the physical world affects our mind, so does our mind in turn affect our physical form. In the world of meditation, this form of comprehensive concept is called body sensation.

Think about the last time you were happy. In addition to being mentally excited, how did you feel on a physical level? Were you in pain? Did you find it difficult to move? Or did you feel uncomfortable for some reason?

Chances are you don't feel this - why? When you're happy and relaxed, you don't feel physically unwell. In fact, you feel lighter and more physically relaxed. At the same time, the exact opposite happens when you are dealing with some sort of emotional upset. For example, you may feel nauseated or uncomfortable if, for example, you panic before a major exam. Or you may feel listless when you are depressed or dealing with massive amounts of mental stress. Your body is a reflection of your mind. When you feel happy, your body is also happier, and you have more rest. While, when you are upset, your physical form tends to manifest in a way that reflects that negativity.

As you prepare to practice meditation, one of the things you want to make sure is that you are working on your ability to understand what your body is saying to you. The easiest way to do this is by practicing body sensation. Body sensors not only allow you to control your central nervous system and allow your mind to achieve a deeper form of mental and physical relaxation, it is also known to increase your body's natural resilience. This work will help you develop your ability to experience a more solid and constant sense of wholeness and well-being, in a way that is not attached to your external obstacles.

Emotional Focus

As you prepare for your meditative journey, another factor to consider is Emotional Self Focus. One of the main goals of meditation is to promote self-care. It is even known that meditation itself has extremely therapeutic properties. Emotion-focused therapy is actually a short-term psychotherapy approach that is usually included in most meditative guides. The logic applied here is simple: emotion-focused meditations are designed to identify and clear the participant's innate emotions. This form of elimination of a specific emotion can be problematic for a person's growth and development, because eliminating a specific emotion in its entirety can cause people to develop mental blocks.

Research has shown that emotion-focused therapy helped participants identify with their own self, helping them better manage their emotional experiences. Mental health problems such as depression, complex trauma, etc. have been improved when associated with emotion-oriented meditations, therefore it has been specifically used to help individuals with the internalized stigma of sexual orientation, for example

As you practice using the meditative guides provided, it is important that you focus on trying to achieve a specific goal during the meditative process. This ensures that you focus on self-care and self-awareness. As you get older, you will find that it is much easier to focus on other people's needs than your own. But while this is very common, it just isn't right. Remembering your own needs and feelings is just as important as caring for others. In addition, it is equally important that you make sure that your self-sacrificing mindset does not result in you suppressing your own emotional needs and depriving yourself of the help you need.

Identify And Deal With Physical Pain

Another important factor in preparing for a meditative lifestyle is clarity about where you are working. Let's say you work on dealing with physical pain. You will need to know specifically what type of pain you are trying to deal with. Understanding the basics and depth of your pain will help you choose which meditative guides are most effective for you.

When it comes to dealing with physical pain, it is important that you make a point to understand which pain management technique is best suited for your condition. Body scanning allows a person to mentally 'X-ray' their body, identify their pain points, and then address or heal them.

Another important form of pain management meditation is the mindful movement technique. This technique teaches individuals to use mindful movements, such as standing in a specific pose and then continuing to go through a list of physical actions, including turning your hands and shoulders, stretching your arms, and moving in and out. exhale at specific intervals. This type of targeted breathing is another common pain treatment technique that can help people with relaxation problems and chronic pain.

Physical Distraction

In addition to all this, there are also a multitude of problems that you want to avoid if you want your meditation to run smoothly. For starters, you want to make sure you have the right set-up. This starts with the space where you have chosen to practice your meditation. Other factors to consider are the ambient noise or your point of view from that physical space. So always make sure to choose a quiet, empty space where you can minimize interruptions and let yourself relax. If you can, try to spend some time outside, or at least make sure your space is well ventilated, so you have fresh air before or during meditation. The fresher air you let in, the easier you'll find it to project yourself outside the four walls you're constantly crammed into.

Soft, quiet beats and musical rhythms, such as ambient music or simple instrumental songs, work well to create a relaxing space. There are also meditative songs and music selections available online on popular streaming sites. These are specially formulated to add an extra level to your meditative depth.

Build Focal Points

Another extremely important part of the meditative process is finding the true meaning of your mind. In general, meditation practices ask you to establish an intention before starting a session. This allows you to fully appreciate and use your meditative time. You can pre-program your meditative focus or intention by using a mental questionnaire process. Start by asking simple questions, such as' Why do I meditate? ',' What do I hope to achieve by meditating? ',' What is my goal? ',' Who am I? ',' What do I want to be? How do I get where I want to be? 'Etc.

The idea here is to use the question to center yourself before you start meditating so that your meditation focuses on that specific point. This is similar to how compasses show you the real north, with a magnet constantly bringing the arrow back to it. Keep in mind that meditation doesn't have to be religious. While certain people meditate to experience God and build upon that consciousness, belief in a higher power does not increase your meditation ability.

Meditation can also be about finding the right wavelength for your thoughts and experiences. However, it is important to keep in mind that although focused meditative instruction seems unnecessary, your meditative energy depends on the mentality with which you begin the meditative guide. Taking time to focus on your intent will not only help increase the efficiency of your meditative guide, it will also help you maximize this time that you take for yourself.

Chapter 12

Creating an Environment for Meditation

Before we jump right into your practice, it's vital that you set yourself up for success. When it comes to meditation, your surrounding is going to be very important, especially if you are just starting out. Remember that as you practice, you'll want as little distraction as possible. You should work on finding a safe space to get started with your mindful meditation. I'll be providing you with some simple tips and tricks to create a space that you can feel relaxed and at peace in.

Step One: Find A "Feel-Good" Space

The very first step for setting yourself up for successful meditation is to choose a room in your house that always makes you feel good. What I mean by this is that you are able to step into this room, take a deep breath and smile to yourself because it brings joy to you. This room should be slightly secluded and quiet. By doing so, you' ll be able to limit the amount of traffic that passes by and noises that could potentially distract you.

When thinking about your space for meditation, mood lighting should be a factor. An example of this would be a room that has a good amount of natural light. It has been said that natural light has the ability to enhance one's mood almost instantly. With that in mind, try finding a room that faces the sun during the time that you decide to meditate. You could also find a view with the sunset or sunrise for a gorgeous backdrop for your meditation.

With your natural light in mind, you don't want the sun blazing on you while you are practicing. If you are indoors, consider dimming the lights to help create a calm sensation within the room. You could also place a sheer fabric over your window to help defuse some of the harsh sunlight if it's shining directly on you. No matter which you choose, you'll want to be able to have options depending on the day.

To take it one step further, you may want to consider a serene paint palette for your room. While the sensory and physical elements are important to consider, you may be surprised to learn how much color can affect your mood. While some say pastel shades are the most soothing, dark colors help individuals feel as though they're returning to the womb. If you have the ability, choose a room color that makes you feel relaxed and calm.

If you feel there is no room in your house that can fit your needs, you could always consider meditating outside! Whether you be on your deck, in your garden, or perched beside a pond; simply find a place that you'll be able to relax your body and soul without too many distractions.

Step Two: Clear Your Mind And Clear Your Space

When you hear distractions, you may instantly think about noise and people talking to you. Having a cluttered area can also be very distracting when you are trying to relax. Once you have chosen your space for meditation, I always suggest having minimal "extras" in the room where you are trying to practice. An example of this may be your office. Often times, we have piles of papers stacked on the desk, filing cabinets that need some attention, and other stressful distractions that can happen in an office such as bills and work.

If you do feel that you need something more in your meditation room, you can always bring in some natural elements. Some people find that they're able to connect better to their mind and body when they're surrounded by nature. If you aren't outside, consider touches of nature that can infuse balance and harmony into your practice. For some, that means jars filled with sand, and for others, it could be a simple vase filled with their favorite flowers.

One of my favorite natural elements in my studio is a water fountain. An indoor waterfall can create soothing sounds that grant the ability to drown outside distractions. Instead, you can close your eyes and pretend you are meditating at the beach. I enjoy matching my breath to the sound of the rushing water; it's something you could consider for your space if you are looking to enhance your meditation area.

Step Three: Aromatherapy And Music

One of the best parts of meditation is that you can create a space that makes you feel joyful and relaxed. A major element to consider for your room of practice could potentially be aromatherapy. There are many different essential oils such as peppermint, chamomile, or even lavender, that can soothe the body, the mind, and the soul.

If essential oils aren't really your thing, there are always incense and candles to burn. These scents have the ability to boost the immune system, eliminate stress, reduce muscle pain, and help create a sense of overall relaxation, too. There is a reason that this form of therapy is becoming more mainstream and gaining momentum. Of course, it's okay to practice without aromatherapy; this is just merely a suggestion as you decide how to begin your practice.

Another element to consider could be music for your space. While it's relaxing for some people, it may not be for you! I find that music can be beneficial for those who live with sirens constantly going off and traffic in general.

As you concentrate on the gentle tones, it can help gain a sense of peace and tranquility. I always recommend music that does not have lyrics. There are sounds such as birds chirping, waves crashing, or wind blowing that you could give a shot. There are many meditation tracks that you can time with your meditation. It may take a few tries, but you are sure to find something you can enjoy during your practice.

Step Four: Fresh Air

While you could include aromatherapy in your meditation room, fresh air will always be the number one factor. There are so many incredible benefits to fresh air that can help you feel refreshed and may help boost your brainpower. If you are meditating indoors, be sure to find a room that has good ventilation. If you find yourself in a room that does not have any windows, you can always consider a standing fan or an air purifier. If this is the case, be sure to find a gadget that is quiet so that it does not interfere with your train of thought.

Step Five: No Technology

I feel is the most important factor to take away when you decide on your space for meditation practice. While of course there are no hard rules when it comes to meditating, you should really consider ditching the technology when it comes down to your time. Aside from your music player, there should be no phones and no computers. There is absolutely nothing more distracting than getting email and text notifications on your phone when you are trying to relax.

What it comes down to is that you are simply taking several minutes to yourself. It's okay to get away from it all for a few minutes. More than likely, those phone calls and text messages can wait a few moments while you spend time meditating and connecting to yourself. It's healthy to unplug from these electronic devices. It may seem difficult at first, but I promise you'll live and may even learn to enjoy some time without being glued to your screen.

With all of this being said, it's finally time to get started on learning your very own meditation practice. We'll be going over everything you need to know about your first meditation. Before you begin, remember to choose your space carefully. The more you practice, the more you'll know how to fine-tune your space for maximum happiness and joy.

Chapter 13
Tips for Meditation

We will share some more suggestions and tips to allow you to continue with your meditation practice. These are not aimed at making you an expert but just to assist you on the journey. It is not necessary to try all of these tips at the same time. You can try one or two at a time to see if they help you. There will be some that work better than others. Find what's right for you.

Begin Your Practice With 2-Minute Sessions

It may sound like it's pointless to meditate for just two minutes but trust us when we say it's anything but. It's simple to do this and is the easiest way for a beginner to learn to practice meditation. Just dedicate two minutes of each day to meditation. Continue this for a week. It's easier to follow through with these two minutes than pressuring yourself to sit still for half an hour. Once you get used to these two minutes, you can add more minutes the next week and so on. You will soon see that you easily meditate at least 15 minutes daily after a couple of weeks, and that will be more than enough time for most. So don't worry and don't make excuses about not having time. Everyone has two minutes to meditate.

Practice Your Meditation Every Morning

A lot of people say that they will meditate every day in the beginning, but most of them fail to follow through with this claim. Don't assume that you will always remember or be inclined to do it. Commit yourself to meditating every single morning after you wake up. After you wash up, just set aside a few minutes for this and you will see how much better your day goes. Early mornings are considered the best time to meditate.

Don't Worry About The Process And Focus On Beginning The Practice

When people start meditating or think about starting it, they often waste a lot of time and energy on worrying about how they should go about it. They waste time in looking up too many methods, finding the perfect mat to sit on, learning chants, etc. All of these are a part of the practice but not the essence of it. You need not spend so much time on this and should try to go with the flow. Just find a comfortable place to sit where you won't be disturbed or distracted by anything. Sitting right on the ground is completely fine and so is sitting on a chair. To begin with, focus less on all this and more on spending two whole minutes just meditating. The stress of these trivial things will hinder your meditation. So try to get more used to meditating itself and worry about all this later.

Pay Attention To How You Feel

Once you begin meditating, you need to try being more attuned to your personal feelings. Pay attention to how you feel and how this practice is affecting your body. Tune in to the thoughts that pass through your mind. Don't focus on them but notice them as they flow past. Be accepting of all the feelings and thoughts that you experience during meditation. Nothing is wrong or right; so, don't judge yourself for any of it.

Count as You Breathe

Breathing is an important aspect of meditation. Find the right place to meditate and then close your eyes as you sit comfortably. Start concentrating solely on your breathing. Focus on your breath as you inhale and exhale. Notice how you take in air through your nose and into your lungs. Pay attention as it leaves your body. When you take in a breath, count one. Count two when you breathe out. Continue the counting as you keep breathing and focus on this alone. It will help you focus more.

It Is Okay For Your Thoughts To Wander

The human mind tends to wander a lot, and you need to be more accepting of it as you meditate. You don't have to assume that you are not allowed to think anything when you meditate. This can be impossible to avoid, at least at first. When you meditate, try not to think but be accepting when thoughts come in. When you notice your concentrating wandering off from your meditation to your thoughts, push back your mind slowly. It can be disappointing, and you might feel like you are doing it wrong, but it is all right. Just slowly come back when your mind wanders away.

Be More Accepting

Like we already said, it is natural for thoughts to appear as you meditate. Don't be defensive and try to push them away all the time. Instead, be more accepting and allow them to come and pass. Take note of these thoughts, and you can focus on them later. But as you meditate, allow them to come and go naturally. Your thoughts are a part of you, and you need to accept and forgive yourself for everything that you are.

Don't Stress About The Method Of Meditation

You might be worried that you are meditating the wrong way at first. A lot of people get stressed about this and think it will be ineffective if they don't practice the right method or do it the right way. The truth is, there is no perfect method of meditation. You can try the various methods we have mentioned and use them as guidelines, but ultimately, you need to do what feels best for you.

Your Mind Doesn't Have To Be Empty While Meditating

Some people think that meditation means getting rid of all thoughts and clearing the mind completely. However, this is not true and can be almost impossible for most people. It can be possible to clear your mind out sometimes, but for the most part, it's not what is essential for meditation. It's normal to have thoughts, and you don't have to force yourself to push them all out. Just be more accepting of them and let them pass without focusing on them. Work more on your concentration, and you will see that it gets easier to reduce distracting thoughts over time.

Take Some Time To Accept Your Thoughts And Feelings

As we mentioned repeatedly, having thoughts while meditating is totally normal. When a thought passes through your mind, it is okay to take a moment and pay attention to it. In the beginning, we recommend to just let the thoughts pass and focus more on breathing. But over time, you can try noticing more of your thoughts too. You should avoid focusing on anything negative and try to bring in more positive thoughts. When you notice your thoughts, you will be able to learn more about yourself. But only allow yourself a moment for this before continuing with your meditation.

Learn A Little More About Yourself Every Day

Meditation is not just about improving your focus or being better able to concentrate. It is about helping your mind develop too. When you become more accepting of your thoughts and feelings, you will learn a lot about yourself. Don't push yourself too hard to think or feel a certain way. Be accepting and learn about yourself. No one can know you better than yourself.

Be Your Own Friend

You need to try learning more about yourself, but this should not be done with a mindset of self-analysis and judgment. Instead, be kinder to yourself. Think of it like learning more about someone you like. Accept who you are and be your friend. Don't be cruel and judgmental towards yourself.

Pay Attention To Your Body

After you get better at counting breaths and meditating, you can try something else. Now you should try focusing on your body. Do this with one body part at a time. As you meditate, focus on a specific body part and try to pay attention to how it feels. Start with the lowest point in your body and move on until every part of your body has been acknowledged. This will allow you to pay attention to your body and learn more about it. You will be able to notice if something feels wrong too.

Be Truly Determined

You cannot say you will meditate regularly and then fail to follow through. It is important to dedicate yourself to this practice. Don't take it lightly. Make sure you stick to this resolution for at least a few weeks. Motivate yourself to follow through with it every day. It will soon become a habit, but not if you lack determination right from the beginning.

Meditate, Regardless Of Where You Are

It doesn't matter if you're on a trip or have to work overtime on some days. Don't skip your meditation practice. You might reduce the amount of time you can dedicate to it, but you should still meditate. You don't necessarily need that meditation corner in your home for this. It can be done while sitting in a car or even while you sit in your office chair.

Use Guided Meditations

It may seem hard to meditate when you first begin. Guided meditations can be instrumental in this case. Use these audio or video files to help you get started. They are very simple and accommodating regardless of whether you are a beginner or have practiced for some time.

Have Someone To Be Accountable To

If you keep your resolution to meditate to yourself, you are less likely to follow through with it. It will be easy to give up because there is no one to berate you over it. This is why you need to have someone that will hold you accountable. It could be a friend or family member. Just keep checking in with them, and they will help you stay on track. You can also find someone to practice it regularly. This could be someone you live with, work with, or even someone who will go to lessons with you. Finding a network of people who are interested in meditation will help in reinforcing your new good habit. These people can help support you through your journey. You can find online forums or communities of people who practice meditation too.

Chapter 14
15 Minutes Guided Meditation (Transcript)

Take your position at the place of your meditation

Be seated

Sit in a completely relaxed manner

Don't do anything immediately

Ground yourself first

Just sit completely relaxed for a few minutes

Get into a comfortable position

Keep your back straight

Ensure that your shoulders are also straight

Your back and neck should be in a straight line

Now, close your eyes

Lean slightly forward and then backward

Lean-to your left side and then to your right

Now, bring yourself to the center and find the best and most comfortable position

Feel your head positioned on your neck

Raise your chin slightly upwards

This will help you in placing your focus between your eyebrows

Try to feel your whole body

Notice if there is tension anywhere

If you feel any part tense, release the tension

Adjust your body to release the pressure

Focus on your breathing

Inhale from your nostril

Hold your breath for a few seconds

Exhale from your mouth

Breathe in

Breathe out

Feel all the tension getting diffused with each exhalation

As you exhale, all the negative energy goes out of your body

It also takes away all the stress

You are feeling joyful and blissed

Simply focus on your breathing

Live in the moment

Remain aware of the things happening around you

As you breathe in your focus on the breath is getting deeper and deeper

You are feeling more and more calm and composed

You smile with every inhalation and feel relaxed with every exhalation

You are feeling blissed out

Now, start paying attention to your breathing

Pay very close attention

Closely observe the path of the breath you take

Become aware of the way it causes your chest to expand

Air is filling your lungs

Then it travels to your gut

It causes your stomach to inflate

You are amused by this act

But you can't release the breath yet

You need to control it

This is your dominion

You are in control

You hold it for a few seconds

Then, release it slowly

Watch the air go out through your mouth

Observe the sound you are making through your mouth

The air is taking away all the tension with itself

The stress in your body is also going away

There are some thoughts in your mind

They don't concern you

But you are drawn to them

Observe those thoughts

Don't get involved with them

Don't interrupt or intrude

Don't judge those thoughts

Simply observe them

Become aware of them

If you run from them, they will come after you

Embrace these thoughts

Accept their presence

Don't be afraid of them

It is time to expand your awareness

Look outside the body

Try to feel the surrounding

Feel the air around you

Become aware of the fragrances

Become aware of the sensation the air is making

Listen closely to any kind of noise being made by the air-conditioning

Expand your awareness even further

Go beyond the realms of the eyes

Look far beyond the limit of your eyes

Try to imagine first snowfall of the season

You are sitting in a comfortable cottage

It is the first snowfall of the season

It is evening now

You are completely relaxed

There is nothing to do

You are looking at the falling snow

You are sipping your coffee

You are in comfortable clothes enjoying the weather

There is nothing to fear

You have the supplies

You have nowhere to go

The family is with you

There is no one to worry about

You can easily sit back and relax

The snowfall has just begun

There is a thin layer of super white snow on the cars

The floor and the roads are not yet fully covered by snow

There is a thin layer of snow on the trees, branches, and leaves

It is giving it a romantic look

You feel a bit of chill

There is a blanket on the chair

You cover your shoulders for more comfort

You are thinking about making a snowman in the morning with kids

You are thinking of the games you'll play with the kids in the morning

It would be a really wonderful sight

The night is approaching

There is a warm bed waiting for you now

You have a book which you are still reading

You start reading the book

But you are drawn to the snowfall

It is the first snowfall of the season

You want to observe it a bit more

You want to cherish this moment

The life is in the moment

Tomorrow this moment would be a past

There would be no way to live it

You leave the book aside

You are now standing firmly in the balcony of your cottage

You light a small bonfire

You want to fill this sight in your eyes

The bonfire is keeping you warm

Some more family members have also joined

They are talking among themselves

But you are lost in the beauty of the snowfall

You want to explore this snowfall further

You go to the back of your cottage

Now, you are watching the snowflakes falling through the window glass

Snowflakes are falling on your windows

You can see them clearly

It is time to sleep

You close your eyes

You fall asleep immediately

It felt like you slept just a few minutes ago but it is morning now

It is a beautiful day

There has been a heavy snowfall whole night

The roads, houses, cars, trees, everything is covered by white snow

Everything is looking mesmerizingly beautiful

You watch is through the window of your room

The kids are not awake yet

You get out to explore the snow

There is a piping hot mug of coffee in your hand

You are standing at the same place you were standing yesterday

A thick layer of snow all around

This is the beginning of the new season

It is a weekend

There is no rush to go anywhere

So, there is no need to clear the snow

No one is shoveling the snow

Everything is calm

There is great serenity in the environment

It is getting complimented by the white blanket of snow all around

The white color is very soothing to the eyes

It is even soothing to the soul

You want to remain in the moment

You want to live this moment forever

It will remain in your eyes now

It is an indelible memory

It is time to become aware of the moment

It is time to feel the breathing

Feel the falling and rising of the stomach

Breathe in

Breathe out

Don't stretch your breathing now

Let it come to a natural pace

Don't put any effort into it

You have been effortless at the moment

You have enjoyed the moment completely

Now it is time to become aware of the surrounding

Feel the warmth or chill in the room

Feel the sensation of clothes on your skin

Experience the air around you

There is no need to open your eyes immediately

You can enjoy the moment a bit longer

Or choose to open the eyes

You are in control.

Chapter 15
Mindful Breathing and Mindful Movement Meditation

Mindful Breathing Meditation

Mindful breathing meditation is the most basic form of meditation for beginners to start their meditation journey. However, basic doesn't mean shallow or easy. Meditation of breath is a powerful and effective tool.

The exercise:

1. Choose a straight sitting position that is comfortable for you. Sit comfortably in a chair or on the floor. Keep your spine straight, but not stiff, and keep your back away from the back of the chair. If it makes you comfortable, then close your eyes. Sit in a place with a comfortable temperature and ensure you won't be disturbed for the next 10 minutes or so.
2. Keep your attention on your breathing. Remember, if your mind wanders off to other thoughts, don't judge or criticize yourself. Let go of any ideas of

achievements or success. Whatever happens, allow it to happen.

3. Focus on your breathing. Feel your breath as it enters your body. Feel your out-breath as you exhale. Feel your belly or chest falling or rising. Feel the air moving in and out by placing your hand on your belly. When you have accurately found the place where you can feel your breath comfortably, focus there, and allow your hands to rest. Let the breath flow at its natural depth and speed. Just breathe normally, your breath may gradually deepen or slow down, or may remain steady – either way is fine.

4. Slowly bring your mind back to your breathing: When you are trying to focus on your breathing, your mind may drift off into different thoughts, fantasies, dreams, feelings, plans, and ideas. This is totally normal, and when this happens, observe where your mind went, don't try to judge it or analyze it, and gently guide your mind back to your breathing. Your mind drifts off and you bring it back to your breathing is an integral part of your meditation. If you start to get annoyed or feel frustrated, take a deep breath and smile. Then refocus your attention to your breathing, just like turning a car into another direction.

5. After 10 -20 minutes of practice, open your eyes and notice how you feel after the meditation. Avoid negative thinking such as 'I am doing it wrong, ' or I can't get it.' Each mindful practice and experience is different.

Stay with the things and events just as they are, from moment to moment.

Practice daily for 10 -20 minutes. Practice different times of the day and see what effect it has on you.

Practice Mindful Movement Meditation

Unlike popular belief, your body doesn't have to remain still to exercise mindfulness meditation. Some meditation practice requires you to stay still for a few minutes. However, almost everybody enjoys and comfortable mindfully moving their bodies. Practice this simple mindful movement meditation and see how you feel afterward.

The exercise:

1. Start with mindful standing: Just stand up straight and place your feet about hip-width apart. Keep the knees a little loose, chest comfortably open and the shoulders back and down. Allow your hands to hang by the side of the body. Make sure your head is perfectly stable in your shoulders and neck. Picture a balloon is on the top of your head, and it gradually drags you upright. If it makes you comfortable, and help you to maintain balance, then keep your eyes closed.
2. Observe the sensation of your breath, feel the sensations in your body, and feel the weight of your body on your feet. Notice the spot on your body that feels uncomfortable, stressed, or tense without trying to relax them.

3. When you are ready, move the arms up and down with your breath. As you inhale, move the arms upwards in front of you and back down again as you exhale. Focus on the sensations in your hands and arms while you repeat 10 times.

4. The next time you inhale, lift your arms in front of the body, then as you exhale, open the arms outwards. As you inhale, bring your arms together in front of your body again. Bring your arms to your sides again as you exhale. Practice for 10 times.

5. Now lift your arms above the head and feel the stretch. See how far you can stretch yourself without difficulty. Stay with the stretch until you start to feel uncomfortable and see if you can stay with the feeling of uneasiness and for a few moments before returning to the pose. Repeat the practice if you feel comfortable with the pose. Keep breathing normally, and no need to hold your breath.

6. Rotate the shoulders slowly a few times in both directions. Notice if you can feel any tension. Simultaneously, feel your inhales and exhales if you can.

7. Gradually switch your head from side to side. Slowly lower your left ear towards your left shoulder.

8. Then gently turn your head in front of your body. Make sure your right ear is aligned with your right shoulder, then go back to the center pose again.

9. Shake your arms and legs for about 30 seconds and finish. Stand and feel the sensation all over your body.

Chapter 16
Mindfulness Meditation

When you enter mindfulness meditation, you become like a mountain. You are surrounded by movement and changes, but you remain just as still and strong. Your thoughts would then be like clouds that float over you. They are there but you do not interact with them; they merely pass you by until they fade away into the distance.

Mindfulness meditation in the formal sense can be practiced daily, but just like exercise and eating you need to set aside specific time for it. However, unlike the first two, you do not have to change into a different set of clothes or prep some ingredients to practice. You can start anywhere and anytime.

How to Apply the Right Meditation Posture

It is important to make sure that you follow proper posture while being still for several minutes. Here are the steps on how to properly position yourself for meditation.

Sitting on a chair

Sitting still for a certain period requires good posture not only for health, but for comfort as well. Slouching, after all, is the surest way to cause long term damage on your spinal cord. Here are some tips on how to improve your sitting posture for meditation:

- Make sure to sit on a chair that will enable you to put your feet flat on the ground. If the chair is too low or high, you would be better off sitting on the floor.
- If you have a slouching problem, you can place wooden blocks or old magazines beneath the two back legs of your chair to allow it to tilt forward slightly. This slight tilt will compel you to maintain a straight back to keep balance.
- Visualize that you have a string pulling your stomach forward until your spine is naturally straight without any feeling of strain. Allow your head to lift naturally until all the discs in your spine are naturally aligned.

- You may place your hands on your knees. They can be facing downwards, upwards, or to the side. You can also place a cushion on your lap and place your hands on top if you feel tension on your shoulders.

Sitting on the floor

The more traditional and formal sitting practice for meditation is on a cushion on the floor. There are two basic postures for that: the kneeling posture and the Burmese posture. It is best to invest in a good quality meditation stool with a flat cushion (called a zafu) on top so that it can absorb the pressure of your weight instead of the back of your legs.

To properly do the kneeling posture, here are some tips:

- Always shake and stretch your legs as well as rotate your ankles before you go to the kneeling posture. This will minimize feelings of tension or strain.
- Prepare the kneeling stool and cushion on the floor, then carefully sit back down on it. Shift your weight until it is evenly distributed.
- Gently straighten your back and place your hands on your knees or lap.

To do the Burmese posture, here are the steps:

- Do some stretching exercises for the legs to prepare them for the position.
    - Lay out a mat or blanket on the floor. Over it, place a firm, flat cushion on which you will be sitting.
    - Carefully lower yourself over the cushion into a sitting position. Try to let your knees to touch the floor; if they do not, you may need to add more cushions until they do.
    - Let your left heel touch or be as close to your right inner thigh as possible. Let your right leg be in front of your left leg with its heel directed at the lower left leg. You do not have to position this perfectly, so adjust according to what is comfortable and stable for you.

- Gently allow your back to become straight, but with your shoulders relaxed. You may then place your hands on your knees or on a cushion on your lap.

Aside from following proper posture, it is important to make sure to meditate during the times when you are not hungry or too full. Otherwise, you will be too distracted or sleepy.

That said, let us move on to one of the most fundamental mindfulness meditations, mindful breathing.

Mindful Breathing Meditation

Mindful breathing meditation is the core of all mindfulness meditation exercises. It is in fact the first thing you usually do to enter the state of mindfulness before you proceed with walking mindfulness, eating mindfulness, and other mindfulness exercises.

Beginners are highly encouraged to practice this every day for at least two weeks so that they could get into the habit of meditation.

If you do not want to get lost in time or be worried about how long you are meditating, you can set a timer on your phone or alarm clock to signal you when to come out of the meditation. It is best to set a gentle tone on the alarm instead of a ringing one, as you would want the reminder to be gentle rather than a disturbance. You can start with 10 minutes, if you like.

Here are the steps to mindful breathing meditation:

Step 1: Get yourself into a comfortable sitting posture, be it in a chair or on the floor. Give yourself time to become stable and comfortable.

Step 2: When you are ready, announce to yourself and the universe that you are ready to focus on the present moment. You may start by saying out loud, "I am in the present moment. I am ready to meditate." Invite an attitude of kindness, curiosity, and acceptance.

Step 3: Shift your focus towards your nostrils. Notice the feeling of your natural breath as you inhale through your nostrils. Then, trace the sensation of the breath as it flows down through your windpipe into your lungs, causing your belly to expand. Notice how it flows out of your belly, causing it to deflate, and then goes back up through your windpipe and nostrils. Continue to focus on this sensation for as long as you like.

Be careful not to change how you are breathing as your purpose here is not to judge how you are doing it. Rather, it is a mere observance of your natural breath, the core of your present moment.

Step 4: As you continue to focus on your breath, you may soon notice your mind wandering off. This is completely normal and should not cause you to worry. All you need to do when you notice this happening is to draw your focus back towards your nostrils.

Each time you start to entertain thoughts unrelated to the sensation of breath, call to mind the word "thinking…" You can also make it more specific, such as "worrying…" or "planning…" or "ruminating…"

After the thought floats away, ground yourself back towards your breath.

Once you hear the timer go off, you can either gently come out of the meditation but bring the state of mindfulness with you throughout the rest of your day. Some like to shift their focus from their breath towards their surroundings after mindful breathing meditation. They focus on the colors, textures, and shapes, the sounds they hear, and so on. This enables them to become more in tune with the present moment than ever.

Guided meditation

The mindfulness meditation practices may be difficult at first. It is recommended to try one of the apps or programs listed in the resources to introduce you to meditation and help you with your posture, breathing and techniques. This will allow you to build a meditation habit with less than 10 minutes a day.

Try practicing mindful breathing meditation right now. If you don't have much time or can't sit down, just pause and take a few breaths in and out focus on your breath.

After you are finished, you might like to learn another type of mindfulness meditation called Walking Mindfulness.

Mindfulness Exercise

Mindful Breathing

You can try short meditation and mindful breathing anywhere; you don't have to be sitting down to try it.

To start focus on breathing in through your nose and focus on the air going in at your nostrils, just focus on this point. Then breath out through your mouth, focus on the air just as it leaves your lips.

Count 1 when you breathe in and 2 when you breathe out, keep counting until 10.

You can also try the full mantra from the smiling meditation mentioned earlier or just the first 2 lines as you breathe in and out:

As I breathe in, my mind becomes calm.

As I breathe out, my mind becomes clear.

Let go of thoughts, worries and things you need to do and just focus on your breathing. You don't have to do this for very long but if you found it helpful, you can try for longer or do it a few times during the day as you feel you need to calm your mind a bit.

Chapter 17

Meditations with Stones and Crystals

Meditation is a simple matter. Have you ever tried it? If you haven't tried it, rest assured that these guided meditations will be very accommodating and straight forward. A tip for effective meditation is to find your center. What this means is that you have to resolve distractions that may be occurring outside of your body and focus your energy and intentions inward. You may hear a variety of thoughts, checklists, reminders, and so forth, emerge in your mind during your relaxation process and that's okay. It won't matter eventually and as you relax, the thoughts will begin to dissolve as you push past them and continue to find your center.

In the same way that crystals and stones can have an impact on the transformation of your energy, so can meditation. When you enter a meditative state, you are giving your body, mind, and spirit an opportunity to hit the reset button and recalibrate. It doesn't take long to accomplish this and as little as ten minutes a day is enough to powerfully shift your energy into a better balance and healthier state.

Meditation is a powerful tool for healing and alignment, just like crystals and stones, we will bring the two together for an even more impactful healing journey. These guided meditations are step-by-step instructions to help you feel rested, rejuvenated, relaxed, and refreshed. You can use them as often as you need to and each one will use one or more crystals for a specific healing purpose.

Once you have a general overview of simple meditations you can do with these wonderful tools, you can begin to create your own meditations for whatever your needs might be in your everyday life.

Healing Heart Meditation

You will need one or more of the following crystals or stones for this Mediation:

- Clear Quartz
- Jade
- Kunzite
- Malachite
- Rhodochrosite
- Rose Quartz

I recommend using Rhodochrosite or Rose Quartz if you are only using one stone for this meditation. You can use all of them if you are able and adding a piece of Clear Quartz will enhance the power of all of the other crystals and stones used in this guided healing meditation.

This meditation is all about opening the heart and protecting it at the same time. We don't want to be subject to being hurt by being overly compensating. This meditation opens you to living openly from the heart while still maintain a strong capacity for loving the self and standing strong in your ability to be graceful and serene in how you express love to everything and everyone around you.

Find a comfortable position lying on the floor or on a bed or mattress. Make sure that you will be undisturbed and can focus for about 30 minutes for the length of the meditation. Have your crystals and stones within reach so that you only have to reach your hand out to pick them up and place them where they need to go. They should be right next to you when you are beginning your meditation.

1. In your lying position, begin by taking some deep inhales and exhales. As you breathe in, count to ten slowly. Hold your breath for a count of five, and then exhale for a count of ten. Repeat this cycle ten times.
2. After you have connected to your breath, continue breathing normally. Starting at the top of your head, notice any tension that may be stuck around your neck, your forehead, and your ears. Make sure your eyebrows are relaxed. Relax your eyelids, your chin, and your jaw. Let your tongue relax as your breath in through your nose, and out through your nose.
3. Move slowly down the body, looking for more tension to release. Release the shoulders, the chest, and the elbows. Release the arms, hands, wrists, and fingers. Notice any places that you are holding onto and let them melt into release.

4. Continue through your belly, your hips, and low back. Release any tension in your thighs and knees, your calves and ankles. Let go of anything that is tense in your feet and your toes until you are fully released and relaxed into the floor and just breathe in this position for a few moments.
5. Now that you are fully relaxed, pick up your crystals and stones and lay them over your heart chakra. Try to maintain your relaxed state while you do this. You don't even need to open your eyes. Move slowly and gently.
6. Align the stone, or stones at the heart center and encircling it. If you have multiple stones, arrange them all around a large, central stone. It doesn't need to be fancy or pretty, and you should try to keep your eyes closed if you can.
7. With the stones in place, you can now begin to use your original breath cycle to connect with the energy of the stones. Breathe in for ten, hold for five, and breathe out for ten. Repeat this cycle five times and let the energy of the stones connect to you. Feel their vibration as you lift them up on your chest with your breathing.
8. Imagine as you are doing this that the stones are radiating soft pink and green light that is gently swirling around your heart. See the light filling your heart.
9. As the light expands in your heart, let it fill your chest. Continue breathing and see the light extending and growing int your head and through your whole torso. Watch the light fill your hips, legs, and feet.

10. As this colorful light fills you, see it reaching outside of your skin and enveloping you, like a soft, warm blanket of pink and green hues. Hold this image in your mind as you continue to breathe and relax.

11. Bring your focus back to the stones and feel their weight on your chest. Since the healing light of the crystal energy all around you and repeat the following mantra in your head, or aloud if you feel comfortable doing so:

"I am open to living a life of love and compassion.

I am strong and capable of loving all of myself, no matter what.

I will always give love to others who are in need, as well as to myself when I am in need of love.

I am open-hearted, caring, and tender and will offer my kindness and support whenever I can if it is a feeling I am inspired to offer.

I have the right to love and be loved.

We are all in need of love and put the energy of love into the Universe with my heart open."

12. Allow yourself to smile softly and bring your focus up to your crown chakra. Feel the light surrounding your body collect inside of you and begin to leave your body through the crown chakra, infusing the Universal energy around you with healing love and light.

13. Take a few more deep breaths and meditate for as long as you need to with their energetic feeling. When you are ready, you can begin to remove the stones from your chest and breathe a few more times before getting up.

14. To enhance the energy that you have just shifted inside of yourself, continue to do tender and loving things for you and others throughout the day. Take a day off of work and go for a walk in the park. Make a soothing cup of tea and enjoy your garden. Talk to an old friend or loved one over the phone or in-person and have a nice connection. Take a soothing and relaxing bath.

You can modify this Heart Healing Meditation as you get more comfortable and experienced with it. You may find new ways to creatively visualize the healing experience. Have fun with it and open your heart every day!

Chapter 18

Morning Affirmations Meditation

Are you looking to start off your day on the right side of the bed? If you want to wake up energetic and ready for any day ahead of you, I highly suggest starting your day off with a morning meditation, topped off with some positive affirmations to get you in a positive mindset.

Of course, you can listen to this meditation at any time of the day, but it is a perfect start to your morning and will only take a small amount of time to energize you and get you started!

As we start this meditation, I now invite you to go ahead and take some deep breaths. With each breath you take, allow the airflow to begin to energize you. Inhale deep into your lungs and exhale everything out.

Breathe in…and exhale. Allow for your breaths to be slow, deep, and calm. Each breath you take brings in the air that your body needs to help get you started. Allow your breaths to fill you with energy and let go of any fatigue you may be feeling at this moment. For the next few moments, this is all I want you to focus on. Just concentrate on your breath. It does not matter what tasks you have for the rest of the day. All you need to think about is breathing in, breathing out, and getting your energy set up for the day.

(PAUSE)

You are going to be ready for this day ahead of you. Breathe in positive energy and allow all positive thoughts to enter your mind. With your next few exhales, let any negative feelings go. If you feel any tension built up in your body, let that go too. You do not have the time nor the energy to waste on negativity. There is only energy and positivity right now. Breathe and remind yourself to be positive.

(PAUSE)

Now, I want you to squeeze your hands into fists gently. As you do this, feel as the muscles strengthen in your arms and your shoulders. Feel now as the strength and energy begin to flow through your veins. You are powerful, and you can accomplish anything you want to. You are capable of accomplishing anything that you need to get done today. You can do anything you put your mind to. Now, relax your fists, and allow your muscles to relax.

(PAUSE)

As your body begins to awaken, feel how warm and energetic you are starting to feel. If you would like, try to open and close your hands a few times. I want you to become mindful of how wonderful your body feels as it wakes up, ready to tackle anything that comes at you today. Allow yourself to become excited for the day, ready for anything that can happen today; there are so many possibilities. Feel now as this positive energy waves through your body and allow your mind and soul to become alive.

(PAUSE)

If you are feeling up to it, I now invite you to enjoy a gentle stretch to get your muscles going. Go ahead and place your fingertips together and gently stretch your arms above your head. Reach for the ceiling and feel the soft pull down your shoulders and into your sides. If you want, gently lean from side to side and feel as your muscles begin to warm up. When you are ready, bring your arms back down and bring your awareness to your toes. Take a deep breath and allow the energy to surge through you.

(PAUSE)

Next, I want you to start to wiggle your feet a little. As you flex your feet, feel as the muscles in your legs enjoy a gentle stretch. Go ahead and spend some time waking your legs up. They are well rested from the night before and are ready to be put to work! Now, hold your feet still and enjoy the sensation of energy tingling through your toes, into your ankles, and up your legs. Take another deep breath in and allow for these sensations to wash over your whole body. The more you move, the more energetic you begin to feel.

(PAUSE)

Now that your body is awake and feeling energetic, it is time to open your mind to positive thoughts to carry you through the day. In the next few moments, we will go over some self-esteem affirmations to boost your confidence and get you excited for the day ahead of you. If, at any point in your day, you feel your stress and anxiety start to take over, I invite you to take a few moments to breathe and repeat the following affirmations to yourself.

As I say the following affirmations, I invite you to continue to focus on your breathing and stretch; however, you feel fit. If you still feel tense in some areas, go ahead and stretch these areas out. This is your time; use it to your advantage. If you start your day off on a positive note, it can get better from there, even if you hit a couple of rocky patches. Feel free to repeat after me or simply listen to the following; it is completely up to you.

I am capable of achieving anything that I work hard for.

(PAUSE)

When times get tough, I have the ability to work through them.

(PAUSE)

I deserve to be happy.

(PAUSE)

I am a strong individual, and I am in charge of my life, even when I cannot control the circumstances.

(PAUSE)

I am worthwhile, even when people make me feel like I am not.

(PAUSE)

I accept myself for who I am.

(PAUSE)

I am proud of all of my hard work and accomplishments.

(PAUSE)

I deserve happiness because I work hard for it.

(PAUSE)

I have many wonderful qualities.

(PAUSE)

I love myself.

(PAUSE)

I am grateful for my life.

(PAUSE)

I am grateful for all of this energy I am feeling.

(PAUSE)

I am ready to tackle this day and anything that comes my way.

(PAUSE)

I will handle everything with as much grace as possible.

(PAUSE)

In tough times, I will remember to breathe and remain calm.

(PAUSE)

I am in control of my thoughts and my body.

(PAUSE)

I choose to be calm and peaceful throughout the day.

(PAUSE)

I am ready to get started with this day and will remember to be at peace.

(PAUSE)

Fantastic. As we draw this meditation to a close, take a few more moments to breathe on your own time and focus your thoughts and intentions for the day. When things become overwhelming, remember to find your breath, and you can work through just about anything. At the end of the day, it all comes down to your mindset, and by starting with this meditation, you are ready to overcome anything with positivity. Now, breathe and get ready to start your day.

(PAUSE)

Meditation Time: 40 Minutes

Breathing Awareness Meditation

Before we begin this meditation, I now invite you to find a position that is comfortable for you. As you settle in, take a few moments to make sure all distractions such as your cellphone and laptop are closed. For the next few minutes, I would like you to just focus on yourself. As you meditate, there is nothing else that matters. If you are feeling anxious right now, that is perfectly okay. We all go through these feelings. What matters right now is that you do something about it.

(PAUSE)

As you settle into position, go ahead and take a nice, deep breath in. If you would like, allow for your eyes to begin to flutter closed. If you are not comfortable with this, simply keep them open and start to soften your gaze. When you are comfortable, all I would like you to do is find your breath. With each breath you take, simply become mindful of how it feels to breathe in fully and exhale everything out. When we feel anxious, we often forget the very basic concept of breathing. Our thoughts begin to move quickly, and our breathing patterns begin to match. Perhaps you are mindful of this, but most likely, you had no idea because you were so focused on being anxious, and that is okay! Just breathe and tune your focus in on yourself.

(PAUSE)

Right now, all you need to focus on is the air entering through your nostrils. It does not matter why you feel anxious, and it does not matter what tasks need to be completed once this meditation is finished. Allow for all of the thoughts in your head to exit and focus only on your breath.

(PAUSE)

On your next breath, I want you to become mindful of how the air travels into your lungs and allow for your belly to expand fully. As you breathe out, feel how your belly gets smaller, and the air moves peacefully back out through your mouth or nose. You may notice that you inhale, feels different from your exhale. Breathe in and feel the comfort of the cool air as it enters your body and how warm it feels as it leaves.

(PAUSE)

If you ever become distracted during your practice, that is perfectly okay. We all get distracted sometimes. If you find yourself getting distracted by noise or thoughts, allow these to pass without judgment and bring your focus back in yourself. There is no need to change anything right now. All you are doing is relaxing and breathing. Simply bring your attention back to your breath and continue a few more moments to breathe on your own.

(PAUSE)

If you would like, you can count with me as you continue to find your breath. On your next breath, I invite you to hold the breath for a few beats. Allow for the air in your lungs to nourish your body and your thoughts. I want each breath to relax you and clear your mind of all worry. When you are ready, we can begin.

Breathe in softly…and hold for one…two…three…and slowly release. Excellent.

Let's do that two more times together.

Breathe in softly…and hold for one…two…three…and release.

(PAUSE)

Breathe in…and hold for one…two…three…and slowly release.

(PAUSE)

Wonderful. At this point, you are probably already feeling much better. Go ahead and take a few more breaths on your own time.

(PAUSE)

During times of anxiety, I want this to be the first practice that pops into your mind. While breathing is a simple task, it can be highly effective. We all experience anxiety in different ways. If you start to become overwhelmed with tasks or emotions, take a step back and find your breath. With each breath you take, gently remind yourself that these feelings will pass, and as long as you are breathing, you are going to be okay. When you are ready, we can continue to the next meditation to keep working through overcoming your anxiety.

Chapter 19

Meditation for Anxiety Under Pressure Script

While there are many different reasons people experience anxiety, being under pressure can be one of the major culprits. Through meditation, you can teach yourself how to remain focused and calm; even when placed in a high-pressure environment. Whether you are giving a presentation, being tested, or even attending a job interview; you will be able to stay calm, cool, and collected when you need to be the most. Next, you will be provided with a meditation script to help you build your relaxation skills for moments you need to be calm.

For this meditation, you will only need to set a few minutes aside. This is a great aspect as you can remind yourself of this script when you only have a few moments to get your mind back into a calm headspace. In the following script, you will be provided with three different ways to help calm your thoughts, relax your muscles, and become mindful of your breathing. All three of these aspects are important so that you can get back to business without the distraction of any panic or anxiety.

To begin this exercise, be sure that you are comfortable. Wiggle your body a bit and loosen everything up. Once you feel you are mindful of your comfort, bring your concentration to your breathing. How does your breath feel right now before you change anything? Allow yourself to take note and gently let go of that thought without judgment.

Right now, I just want you to focus on your breathing. Breathe in softly and let it all go. Breathe in nice and deep, take all of that oxygen in, and then let it back out. When you can, try to slow your breathing down. With each breath you take, try and count it out to the number of four and then hold that breath for three before letting it out on the same count. When you are ready, try this with me.

And, breathe in…4.3.2.1

Brilliant. Try that a few more times until you feel you are completely in control of your breath.

Breathe in…4.3.2.1…hold…and exhale…4.3.2.1

Very good. Focus on your breath. I don't want you to think about anything else in the moment. It's just you and your breath, nothing else.

Breathe in… …and exhale…

With each breath you take, you can feel a sense of calmness washing over you. Each breath is bringing the focus back into your brain. You are relaxed and comfortably alert. With each breath, you are teaching yourself that you can, and you will be relaxed under pressure. There is nothing that can shake you. You are strong and one with yourself. There is nothing that can take that away from you.

Great.

Now, I would like to invite you to bring your new-found focus to your muscles. How is your body feeling right now? I want you to be mindful of how your jaw feels; how your shoulders feel; and now how your hands feel. When we are under pressure and stressed, we often hold all of our tension here.

Now that you are aware of the tension, allow yourself to unclench your teeth. Allow for your jaw to fall slightly slack into a comfortable position. Remove the tongue from the roof of your mouth and take a nice, deep breath in. Feel already how relaxed you feel now that your jaw isn't clamped shut.

With that in mind, lower your shoulders from your ear. If you would like, gently roll them forward and back; allow for the muscles to fall loose. Again, feel how this new position is already helping you feel much calmer and relax. Your body appreciates when you become conscious of putting yourself in a more relaxed position.

Finally, bring your attention back to your hands. Are they clenched and tight right now? Allow them to fall open and relaxed. Your arms can rest by your side with no tension. There is no need for any of that right now. You are in a safe environment. You are being mindful of making yourself calmer. You are using your skills to relax under any type of pressure thrown at you.

Now, bring your focus back to your breathing. On your own time, run a body scan that you learned earlier. Are there any other spots of tension you are holding onto? If yes, direct your calm energy toward those areas and release the tension. There is no need for it. It's just you and your breath right now; nothing else.

Relax your body. Relax your mind.

Whenever you are under pressure, remind yourself to breathe. When you have power over your mind, you have power over any event that is thrown at you. As long as you stay calm and remember to breathe, you can get through anything.

Relax your body. Relax your mind. Remember to breathe.

When you are ready, take a few more deep breaths before returning your thoughts to your surroundings. Remember that you are in control. Just remember to breathe.

Chapter 20

Positive Body Image Script

Let's face it; there is always something that we don't approve of on our bodies. I 'm here to tell you that you absolutely need to stop being so hard on yourself! Everyone else out there is judging you, stop being mean to yourself. You have a heart in your chest, you have lungs that keep you breathing, and you have a body that allows you to get through life. It's time to appreciate everything that you have instead of fretting over the things you don't.

In the following meditation, we will focus on self-image and self-acceptance. Now is the time to learn how to love yourself. When you are ready, we can begin.

As you settle into your meditation space, I want you to find the most comfortable position possible. It doesn't matter what has happened before this moment nor what is going to happen after. Right now, there's you and this moment. Make yourself comfortable and allow for your mind and body to relax.

Before we begin, take a moment to take note of how you are feeling right now. How are you feeling? How is your body feeling? Take another few seconds and scan your body, starting from your toes and gently bring your focus up your feet, over your ankles, up your legs, and continue scanning up over your stomach and your chest, take that focus over your shoulders and neck and face.

Where are you feeling tense? Where are you feeling relaxed? Remember, there is no point in judging yourself right now. You are simply just becoming mindful of your body; there is no need to change anything right now. Notice as you become aware of the areas of tension, you are able to relax them with little to no effort. By simply being mindful, you allow your body to relax. Your muscles are becoming less tense and loose all on their own. All you have to do is sit there and relax. You're not even trying. With each passing moment, your body realizes that you are safe, and it's okay to let down your guard.

If you are feeling up to it, I would now like to open a conversation about your body image. The question here; what is body image? Perhaps the first thing that pops into your mind is what you feel your body should look like. Maybe you want a bigger butt or smaller hips or a bigger bust. That is okay. But, what does body image mean to you? Consider all of the ideas and thoughts you have about your own body. Take a second to take note of how those ideas and thoughts make you feel. Perhaps you are accepting of your body or maybe even comfortable. Some may feel dissatisfied and unhappy, and it's perfectly okay to feel however you are in this moment. There is absolutely no judgment, just a sense of being mindful of your body and mind.

Now, I want you to take a moment to consider accepting your body for everything that it is. What if you stopped wasting energy on hating aspects of your body and feeling perfectly okay about your physical self?

Bring your focus to your breath and think about what that would feel like if you could finally accept yourself. When was the last time you felt happy about your body? What part is the easiest for you to accept?

I want you to picture your body as a whole. You're not a collection of different parts. I want you to picture loving your mind, your body, and your soul. You are a collective person, and it's healthy to love yourself!

True, these thoughts can be difficult, but you can take a step back from facing these ideas head-on and take a few moments to relax. If at any point you feel overwhelmed, go ahead and breathe in deeply and allow all of the negative energy out with your next breath. Relax your mind, notice your breath, and center your thoughts.

If you feel tense anywhere in your body, allow the muscles to relax. With each breath you are taking, you can allow your body to relax and let go of tension. You are perfectly safe in this moment. No matter what your thoughts are on your body right now, it's okay.

Once your body is relaxed, and you are ready to start up again, I would like to go over some positive body image affirmations. If you would like, you can listen or repeat them to yourself. All you need to do in this moment is relax and allow yourself to be mindful and calm. When you are ready, we can begin.

It's okay for you to accept yourself the way you are.

Your body is beautiful.

Your soul is beautiful.

Your mind if beautiful.

You are wonderful the exact way you are.

There is nothing you need to change about your body.

You are a fantastic person.

It's okay to love the skin you are in.

Any imperfections you have make you, you.

You are healthy.

You are whole.

You are human.

It's okay to accept your imperfections.

You are human, and imperfections are a part of life.

You do not need to judge yourself.

You can use your energy to be positive.

It's okay to accept yourself for who you are.

You love your body.

You love your mind.

You love your soul.

Great. Now, after a deep breath or two, I would like for you to repeat after me.

It's okay for me to accept myself the way I am.

My body is beautiful.

My soul is beautiful.

My mind is beautiful.

I am wonderful the exact way I am.

There is nothing I need to change about my body.

I'm a fantastic person.

It's okay to love the skin I'm in.

Any imperfections I have make me, me.

I'm healthy.

I'm whole.

I'm human.

It's okay to accept my imperfections.

I'm human, and imperfections are a part of life.

I do not need to judge myself.

I can use my energy to be positive.

It's okay to accept myself for who I am

I love my body.

I love my mind.

I love my soul.

Go ahead and repeat these until you believe them. Once you do, take note of how these positive affirmations make you feel. What does it feel like to believe in your own self-worth and to accept yourself for how you are? Allow these thoughts to pass and kindly return your thoughts to your breath. Remember that there is nothing to worry about right now. All that matters in this moment is you and your breath — nothing else.

When you are ready to return to your day, gently bring your focus back to your surroundings. You are becoming aware of your body, relaxed in position. Listen to the world as it gently begins to buzz around you. I hope that you now feel centered and relaxed. Remember to love yourself and accept yourself for who you are. As you repeat these affirmations, you will begin to believe in yourself and lead a happier life.

Chapter 21
Self-Healing Scripts

In short notice, sometimes, all we have is ourselves. If you need a few moments to step back and breathe in times of emotional and physical pain, the following meditations are going to be perfect for you. We will start out with simple healing and relaxation meditation and end with a guided morning starter complete with some daily affirmations. When you are ready, we can get started on learning how to self-heal.

Healing and Relaxing Meditation

Before we begin this first meditation toward self-healing, I invite you to create a comfortable space for yourself before we even begin. Go ahead and set yourself up in a safe space with zero distractions. For some, this may involve your favorite yoga mat, some peaceful music, or even a relaxing candle burning. I want you to create your space; however, makes you feel the best. Once this is complete, we can begin our meditation.

As you settle into your practice, go ahead and find a comfortable position. I want you to allow yourself to relax in this position, whether you are sitting or lying down. Now that you are feeling your body begin to relax go ahead and bring your awareness to your breathing. I would like to go ahead and just spend a few moments doing this. All you have to do is breathe.

(PAUSE)

With each breath, I want you to imagine that you are breathing in cleansing air. Allow for each breath you take to wash away the tension you have been holding in your body. If you feel some areas are tenser than others, go ahead and take a gentle note. From this point on, we will address these areas, and work on healing our body, healing our soul, and healing our mind. Good. Just breathe and let it all go.

(PAUSE)

Now, with your next breath, I invite you to close your eyes and begin to imagine a wave working its way toward you. This is a comfortable wave, filled with healing powers and gentleness. The water is warm and comfortable as it gently makes its way over to you. Now, picture the wave beginning to kiss your toes and gently washes over your feet. Perhaps this wave gives you a tingling sensation or how it feels to step into a warm bath. Allow for the relaxation to softly wash over your feet and up over your ankles. Take a deep breath in and enjoy this feeling of relaxation begin to take over your body.

(PAUSE)

Picture now that the wave is slowly working its way up your lower legs, over your upper legs, and begins to spread its way further up your body. How does this relaxing wave feel? Allow for it to rise up over your hips and gently caresses around your stomach and lower back. Take a few moments here to note how your core is feeling at a time like this. If it is in knots, take a few deep breaths and let it all go. You are in a safe space. This is a time to heal and forget past issues. They do not matter right now. There is just you and the healing power of this wave. Allow for it to wash up over your arms and your chest. Take a deep breath and focus on the healing powers.

(PAUSE)

While this may seem overwhelming for some, remember that this wave is filled with healing powers. I want you to give in to the feeling of relaxation and picture that this wave is now washing over your shoulders, up over your neck, and finally spreads over the top of your head. At this moment, your eyelids may begin to feel relaxed and heavy. I want you to relax and allow your body to let it all go. Notice now how wonderful your body begins to feel as you calm your mind and your body. You are relaxing completely from the crown of your head to the tips of your toes. Allow for the relaxation to spread down from your neck to your spine and into the bottom of your tailbone. You are in a very safe space right now, and you are doing a wonderful job with this meditation.

(PAUSE)

Fantastic. Before we finish up with this meditation, go ahead and take a few moments on your own to breathe. If there is any tension left in your body, picture the healing wave, and allow for it to wash over these areas to take away any stress you may be holding onto. After this meditation, I hope you enter awareness feeling better than before. You have the power to heal your mind and your soul. If you are ever at a loss, tune in to yourself and ask what you need. Sometimes, it's just a few moments of peace and quiet. Now, breathe and let go.

(PAUSE)

Meditation Time: 15 Minutes

Pain Management for Self-Healing Meditation

If you are feeling mental or physical pain right now, realize that you are moments away from finding peace and pain relief. When you are able to relax, this can be a very effective skill for pain management. For individuals who are able to relax through pain, they typically have a higher tolerance for the pain and feel it less. In the next few moments, we are going to go ahead and work through some exercises to help you relax and make that pain go away. When you are ready, find a comfortable position, and we can begin.

As you settle in, I now invite you to begin to become mindful of how you are feeling right now. As you make some mental notes, I do not want you to change anything of how you are feeling or what you are thinking about. Right now, all you need to do is observe your pain, your thoughts, and how these things feel to you. Our pain management begins with becoming aware of these feelings.

(PAUSE)

Now, I want you to take a deep breath in and let the tension go with your next exhale. Where is your body holding onto your tension? For each person, this is going to be different. Some of us hold our stress in our jaws, and others hold it in their shoulders. On a different note, I want you to become aware of the parts of your body that are relaxed at this moment. Where there is bad, you can always find good. Go ahead and take a few moments to take mental notes of where you are tense and where you are relaxed.

(PAUSE)

As we move through the next part of the exercise, I want you to continue to breathe slowly. A major part of pain management is to simply be passive with your attitude. We are not trying to make anything happen right now; it is all about taking notice of how you are feeling. Go ahead and breathe on your own for a few moments and try to let that tension go.

(PAUSE)

Pain is something we all experience. I want you to gently become aware of the pain you have experienced or are experiencing right now. Our bodies are constantly moving and changing. The way we feel in our bodies can change from morning to night. At the end of this meditation, you will feel different than how your body felt in the beginning. All you have to do right now is simply observe how you are feeling and take mental notes.

(PAUSE)

Now, I want you to begin to accept how you are feeling. While pain can be difficult and intolerable, I want you to accept how you are feeling both emotionally and physically. Accept the way you are, whether these feelings are positive and negative. We must accept ourselves for who we are, even in the hard times. Allow your mind and body to be exactly how they are. There is no good or bad; just allow yourself to exist. Breathe.

(PAUSE)

When you are ready, I would like to go through some self-healing affirmations together. You can repeat after me or simply listen to the words I am about to say. This is your practice; you can complete this meditation; however, you see fit. Take a deep breath, and we can begin.

(PAUSE)

At this moment…I am choosing to accept myself.

(PAUSE)

I accept myself…and I accept the pain that I feel.

(PAUSE)

I feel pain…but I will not let this pain define me.

(PAUSE)

I choose to let this pain go…I can be relaxed.

(PAUSE)

I accept myself for who I am and what I feel.

(PAUSE)

Wonderful. With these thoughts in mind, it is time to return to your awareness. I want you to carry these words with you through your day. Any time you feel pain, go ahead and repeat these affirmations to yourself. As you learn to breathe and relax, you will be able to let this pain go and accept yourself the way you are. To finish this practice up, go ahead and take a few more breaths on your own time. Allow yourself to release your pain and return to your day feeling more at peace.

(PAUSE)

Meditation Time: 20 Minutes

Chapter 22

Color Visualization Meditation Script

Do you have a short moment to meditate? This script is perfect for those who just need to take a few minutes out of their day. By visualizing calming colors, you'll be imagining each color of the rainbow so you can take a few moments to relax. Remember to focus your mind and allow yourself to relax into this moment, even if it's only for a few minutes.

Before we begin this script, take a few deep breaths on your own time. As you breathe, begin to draw your thoughts to how your body feels in this moment. Perhaps you are having a stressful day, or it's not going according to plan. That is okay. Try your best not to change anything in this moment. All you need to do is notice how your mind is feeling, how your body is feeling, and accept yourself for how you are in this moment.

As you continue working through your breath, carefully notice that your body is already beginning to relax a bit. Breathe in…and allow for your shoulders to drop from your ears. Exhale and release your teeth from being clenched together. As you become more and more relaxed, your eyelids may even begin to feel heavier.

Good…Now I want to invite you to begin to paint a picture in your mind. To start off, I want you to begin to imagine a shade of red. Once you have the color red in your mind, try to paint your mind with different shades of red. What does the color red remind you of? Try to think of red objects such as sunsets, delicious apples, romantic roses, or anything that comes to your mind. Take note of how the color red makes you feel and allow yourself to relax into this color.

When you are ready, bring awareness to the color orange. Notice how the orange blends from the red and fills your vision. How does the color orange make you feel? As you work through your breath, try to picture some of your favorite orange objects. There are festive pumpkins, delicious carrots, and beautiful orange flowers. Try to envision different shades of orange and enjoy the feeling this color brings to you.

Next, we will bring our awareness to the joyful color of yellow. Take a deep breath in and allow for your vision to be filled with different shades of yellow. Imagine fresh lemons, bright flowers, and the sun warming your skin. There are so many different levels of yellow to imagine, allow it to cleanse your mind with pure joy. Imagine the color yellow filling you up and making you happy.

Now, the yellow is gently going to shift into a green color. Green is often associated with joy as well. There are many different shades of green, especially in nature. I want you to think about beautiful green leaves and grass and plants that you find out in the world. There are gorgeous shades of green; allow the color to fill your vision. As you inhale, take note of how this color makes you feel.

When you are ready to move onto the next color, begin to fill your vision with the color blue. The sky above us is blue, the water in the ocean and the streams and the lake are blue, perhaps your favorite person in this world has blue eyes. Think of what the color blue means to you and allow it to fill your senses. Inhale and exhale; allow this color to fill you with a sense of calm.

Purple is the next color that should begin to fill your mind. There are many beautiful shades of purple that you can find in the sunrise, in flowers, and other objects. Immerse yourself into this color and gently find your breath. Notice now how much calmer your breathing has become now that you have let go of your stress. In this moment, there is just you and your favorite calming colors.

If you would like, return to your favorite color out of the ones we just covered or perhaps select a color that makes you the happiest. No matter what color you choose, allow it to fill all of your senses, and remind you to be relaxed. No matter how bad things get, there is always a different way of looking at it. If you are stressed, close your eyes and remind yourself of your favorite color and the objects associated with that color.

When you are ready, I now invite you to bring awareness back to your surroundings. As you gently open your eyes, notice now how your mind is clear, and your body feels so much more relaxed. Give your muscles a little stretch and jump back into your day with a better sense of peace and joy.

If you enjoyed any of these meditations, you most likely have a very creative mind. Visualization meditations can take practice if the concept is something you're not used to, but it can be incredibly rewarding!

I suggest starting with more basic meditations before moving onto some of the more advanced scripts to follow. Being able to visualize your journey is an important aspect of meditation. When you are able to paint yourself a picture, this means that your mind is open and free to explore spiritual possibilities.

If you feel silly at first, you're not alone! Remember to focus on your breath, and that your practice is your own. Please feel free to customize any of these scripts to your liking. At the end of the day, the only thing that matters is that you are comfortable with what you are doing. As long as you are able to relax and calm yourself, you can benefit greatly from meditation.

Chapter 23
Guided Meditation - 30 Minutes Mindfulness Training

(to be read quite slowly. Increasingly slowly to help bring the more rapid state of waking in line with the rhythmic and slower cadence of breath and sleep)

Welcome.

This meditation is to be experienced lying down in a safe, comfortable and uninterrupted place you can remain asleep once the meditation plays through.

(PAUSE)

Lying down now, give yourself the space to breathe deeply and fully. Allow the breath to enter through your nose, descend along the length of your body and reach your belly which rises in response to the fullness of oxygenated air. It feels SO GOOD to let in this fresh new breath.

As you exhale, let the parts of the day you no longer need rise up and out of your body with your breath, gently breathing out through your mouth, lips shaped into a small "O". Feel the weight of the day leaving your body as you exhale, your belly flattening as the air leaves and pause here in this open space of release.

Good.

Now, breathe again in through your nose, imagining the breath has a color to it, any color of your choosing, the first color that comes to mind. Allow this color to permeate your entire body as you breathe it in through you nose, as the air travels to every single cell, bringing light and warmth, oxygen and peace to your being. You are a being filled with this colored light and infused with the newness of the atmosphere around you, a system of molecules and vibrations always regenerating with its own wisdom. All you must do to be a part of it is to breathe it in. Let it fill you.

Wonderful.

As you exhale, allow everything that no longer serves you to simply rise up and float out of your body through your rounded lips in a nice long exhale. Find yourself noticing the lightness that comes with each breath and release. Feel the peace of letting go the day. The week. The elements in your life you no longer need. How easy it is to simply let them go. How good it feels to breathe in the atmosphere. To take part in the universe. To discover the grace of breath.

Continue now, breathing in through your nose, bringing in light and color and newness and exhaling through the mouth, releasing all that is ready to release.

[1 minute of silence or light music]

Beautiful.

You find yourself feeling lighter by the moment, releasing everything that no longer serves and embracing the expansive wisdom that continually surrounds you, allowing the regenerative nature of the universe to become part of you through breath and rhythm. Through the simple act of breathing. This communion with life all around you. And it feels so good to be part of this rhythm.

Notice also how your body becomes more grounded, more connected to the substrate beneath it, to the earth itself. How you are at once light as air and part of the earth. How you are right where you need to be, in the most perfect place for you right now in this entire universe, supported and free.

And allow yourself to deepen further into this peace. Let any tension remaining in your body, your mind, flow down into the ground, into the core of the earth itself to be transformed and used for other purposes. You do not have to hold onto it any longer. The earth itself knows how to best use the excess energies we do not need.

Feel yourself melt right into the place you are, becoming fluid, becoming more sentient, becoming grace. Movement and light, breath and air. Every part of you now, every cell in your body breathes in the universe around you and breathes out in communion. Breathing becomes– you realize it IS– a conversation. It is a connection. Breathing is BEING life.

You are being. You are life. You are in the perfect place at the perfect time. You are everything you need to be right now.

Your body is pleasurably connected to the fibers beneath you. You notice the pleasant heaviness that comes from the safety of sinking into a warm space, a space you can trust, a space in which you are completed connected, held and supported. With every breath now, you sink deeper and deeper into a state of peace, of ultimate comfort, of knowing your place in the world. It is as simple as this, a noticing of the way you are part of everything around you and the beauty that comes from breathing in the atmosphere and breathing out the colors of your breath to create a resonance that holds and supports you right where you are at; just as you are now.

Every time you exhale now you create a field of light and color around you. Every time you inhale, the light and color become part of you. Every time you inhale, you feel yourself fill with lightness of air. Every time you exhale, you deepen into the fibers below you and the support of the earth itself.

Allow your noticing to grow larger.

Notice how the room around you becomes filled with this positive light and energy that you are breathing in and out. How the energies of the entire universe, how the support and grounding of the earth infuses the space in which you find yourself, and how this changes the space itself. Fills it with more peace, more safety, more comfort, more life and love.

Allow this to expand even further. Notice how this beautiful energy also infuses the entire house or building, the larger area in which you find yourself. How your very nexus, your very center of breathing and imbibing the universe is helping the entire space around you, large and small, near and far, become more infused with loving, peaceful and serene energy. How you create a larger sphere of radiance that surrounds as far as you can see, as far as you can feel, and breathes with you, within you.

(1-minute music/silence)

Ahhhh (sigh type of voice, in order to engage this response in listener, like a long deep exhale). This is the majesty of the living world as it becomes part of you, responds to you, emanates from you. This is the magic of breath and grounding. This is your deepest nature, your connected being, your beautiful soul. At once a part of everything around you and helping to create that which is around you.

Each breath continues to deepen your state of peace and harmony, rest and relaxation, trust and security in the communication you have with the particles of air, the elements of nature, the energies of the universe.

As with a cradle, you are held and supported, loved and carried and can allow yourself to sink deeper into a state of bliss and union, comfort and support.

You notice the colors shift and change, the sounds soften and swell, the concrete pieces of waking life fall away. The world blends and melds with your larger sense of being, with the larger consciousness of the earth, with the wisdom of the universe at large. Your body softens and stretches, settles and soothes. You are fluid and warm, bathed by the universe itself as you drift into a restful state of existence.

Let the rhythm of your breath soothe you. Feel its rise and fall in its most natural state massaging every cell in your body. Massaging the musculature surrounding your skull, releasing the tensions on the bones, your jaw, your eyes, your sinuses and tongue entirely. Feel the sweet release of open space for your mind to flow freely, your head itself swoon. Let your head sway side to side as you continue to unwind down into the neck, releasing even further any aches or pains, any stiffness and tightness, becoming fluid, light, air, becoming oxygen itself flowing through the body, connecting to the space around you.

Let your shoulders drop into the surface beneath you, releasing every bit of weight they carry, and your chest rise and fall easily in the softness you create with your breath. It is as though effortless, your breathing, your releasing, your increasing sense of peace and comfort. This restful state of bliss.

Notice your abdomen soften, with each and every breath, your belly is massaged from the inside out, your entire body can sense the renewed vigor of the cells, so full of oxygen and the softness this release brings. Even your hips roll wide open, released into the rhythm of the breath, the flow of blood and openness of your state of being.

Your low back and legs follow suit, settling into the most comfortable state of repose, rocking slightly with each intake of breath and settling with each outtake until your exhale reaches the very tips of your toes, the base of your feet and sends itself out into the air around you, out into the universe to be recycled, regenerated, and transformed into new energy or matter. You exhale all that you no longer need and inhale the freshness of new breath, the lightness of being, the fluidity of an ever-nourishing universe.

When you inhale again, you revel in the lightness of your body, the sense of being water itself, the motion of being still. You find you are everything that is peaceful about this universe, that you are so satisfied in this state of being. That you have become peace itself.

Your body knows how to best support you. It knows how to hold the attention of deep relaxation while being alert to the world around you. Your mind knows how to heed the call of the body, the need for rest, the ability to transition between states. It knows that when it is needed it will be called upon again, but for now, everything is just fine. There is nothing but this space, nothing but this peace, and a certainty in the wisdom of dreams.

You float and absorb the energies of the womb of life and allow yourself the regenerative nature of sleep knowing that anything important will gain your attention as it needs to, you need not hold onto any ideas or thoughts, they will find you again when it is time.

And in this you drift and know this is a type of home. A connection to the cosmos inside of you and all around you. A colorful and flavorful connection to life that blends with your cells, blends with your neurons and leads you into a blissful form of serenity conducive to sleep.

Breathe now, in and out at your own pace, while the energies of the universe move through you, cleanse you, inform you, hold and support you and allow you the deep healing of rest. Feel the incredible expansiveness and drift of the universe in your cells and in your peaceful body. Allow yourself to sink in.

(Music/sounds to support the transitional state into sleep. Next 15-20minutes)

(Towards ends of the recording, leave with this whispered prompt):

As the music fades you find yourself sinking even deeper into rest. The silence brings you a peace greater than you have known and carries you in sleep for exactly the right amount of time for you.

You breathe and find peace in being.

You are exactly where you need to be.

You are just perfect as you are.

You continue to breathe and release.

As the world too, breathes and unfolds.

Chapter 24

Guided Meditation for Self-Esteem Script

There are too many moments in our life when we are our own worst critics. If you are constantly bashing your body, putting yourself down, or feel you generally have low self-esteem, this script is going to be perfect for you! Through meditation, you can boost your confidence and your self-esteem. When you feel good about yourself, your body will be able to relax and just live life the way it's meant to be.

As always, I now invite you to relax. You will want to find your most comfortable position and allow all of the tension to begin melting away from your limbs. As you find your breath, I want to paint a picture for you. Simply do nothing right now but allow for your breath to become natural.

As you breathe, I want you to picture a staircase in your mind. Right now, you are standing at the top of these stairs. As you look down at the bottom, there is a pool of relaxation and peace. When you are looking down, I invite you to take a mental note of how you are feeling right now.

Take a deep breath and picture yourself taking a soft step down. With this step, you are already closer to the relaxation pool you want to be floating in. Each step you take down, feel how much more relaxed your body is becoming. Your arms are relaxing; your legs are relaxing; your jaw is becoming loose as you step closer and closer to the bottom of the stairs.

One step at a time, you are making your way down the stairs. Your arms are feeling heavier, your legs are heavier, the relaxation is pulling you down gently, and it feels comfortable. You are safe in this moment and slipping into the pool of relaxation will be such a relief. Allow for gravity to pull you down gently.

Feel now as your back and your neck are both relaxing, too. Your shoulders being pulled away from being shrugged up into your shoulders, your eyes becoming heavy with relaxation and every part of your body is becoming calm and relaxed. Go ahead and allow for your mind to drift away from you. Everything is feeling wonderful as you approach the bottom of the stairs.

Now, you are taking the final steps to the bottom of the stairs. Go ahead and admire the pool of relaxation as you gently step in. Allow for your mind to drift as you settle into the calmness of the pool and rest your eyes. Your whole body is loose and relaxed; you haven't a care in the world.

I would like you to allow your mind to drift now. As it does, I would like to go over some positive affirmations for your self-esteem. You can listen to them and repeat them if you would like to. While some may apply to you, others may not. Listen to your mind and your heart as we go over the affirmations. Once we are done, you can allow your mind to continue drifting. Simply breathe, relax, and we can begin.

You are capable of doing so many amazing things with your life.

You are a loving person, and you deserve to be happy.

You are strong, but you do not need to be strong all of the time.

You are worth it.

You have the power to control your emotions.

It's okay to accept yourself.

You need to be kind to yourself.

You are absolutely perfect the way you are in this moment.

It's okay to be happy.

It's okay to be proud of yourself.

Now, repeat after me.

I'm capable of doing so many amazing things with my life.

I'm a loving person, and I deserve to be happy.

I'm strong, but I do not need to be strong all of the time.

I'm worth it.

I have the power to control my emotions.

It's okay to accept myself.

I need to be kind to myself.

I'm absolutely perfect the way I am in this moment.

It's okay to be happy.

It's okay to be proud of myself.

Allow for your mind to drift and repeat these affirmations as needed. You can repeat them until you believe them. These are all true for you, and you deserve to build your sense of self-assurance and confidence. At the end of the day, you will always have yourself. It's up to you to become your biggest cheerleader!

You can, and you will make positive changes in your life. When you increase your self-esteem and gain a positive mindset, you will begin to attract positive events and positive people into your life.

Now, I want you to bring awareness back to your mind. Feel now how much happier and relaxed you feel. Notice how calm you are and take a moment to enjoy this new sensation. Any time you are feeling down on yourself, I want you to repeat these affirmations to yourself. You deserve to feel good. Be in charge of your own happiness.

When you are ready to return to your day, take a few more deep breaths. Gently bring your awareness back to your space and return to your day with positivity and gratitude.

Chapter 25

Guided Meditation: Overcome Fear

Welcome to session one of overcoming anxiety, fear and discontentment every day for 1 week…

I'm honored to guide you through this relaxing session so that you can let go of all doubts that hold you back from attaining the life that you deserve ….

meditation is a wonderful tool for being able to calm the mind and relax the body so that you can think clearly about all that you want to achieve and strive for … in a state of deep relaxation you are able to let go of fear, doubt, and suffering when the art of meditation is practiced on a daily basis …

so let's begin …

making sure you're in a place where nothing will disturb you from the outside world … please take a nice deep breath in and out allowing your eyes to close as you exhale … ensure that you are very relaxed by having your head fully supported and all of your muscles can fully let go as we go along through this session …

continue taking deep breaths in and out counting to 7 breaths as you go along …

breathing in …. and breathing out any worries from your day … 1…

breathing in fresh oxygen …. and breathing out your stress and concerns… 2…

inhaling a new peaceful sense of being … exhaling any tension … 3…

inhale serenity …. exhale troubles … 4…

breathing in that fresh new air … and breathing out anything that holds you back … 5…

inhale peace …. exhale stress … 6…

last one, so make it really full and deep … and breathing out into a nice state of relaxation … 7…

good…

let your breath return to a natural flow now… but try to follow closely along with it… notice how your breath is slowing to a nice rhythm and you body is gently expanding and contracting as you breathe automatically…

(pause)

Now draw your attention to the tips of your toes … notice any sensations in your toes … the temperature … the nearby textures …

(pause)

bring your awareness now to the soles of your feet … notice how the soles of your feet feel …

(pause)

allow for a nice relaxing sensation to begin in the soles of your feet … you can imagine that each time you inhale this relaxation expands … breathe in and let your feet become completely relaxed…

(pause)

now allow this relaxation to spread into your ankles …. notice how good your feet feel when you imagine this comforting feeling …

(pause)

allow for relaxation to travel up into your calves, filling your lower legs with a sense of calm… each breath you take, the relaxation intensifies ….

(pause)

breathing … relaxing … notice how your knees are letting go of any tension … just by placing your awareness on them ….

(pause)

this nice feeling travels up into your upper legs … relaxing your quadriceps … hamstrings … your entire thighs let go of any tension … and sink deeply into the surface that supports your legs …

(pause)

notice how each leg is so very relaxed in this very moment …. can you become aware of any differences between the left leg and the right leg?

I don't know if one is more relaxed than the other … or perhaps one might feel lighter, or heavier … whatever you notice is perfectly fine …

(pause)

imagine that this relaxation is spreading into your pelvis and hips … it is so soothing and so wonderful … you deserve this deep relaxation ….

(pause)

allow for your abdomen to receive this same love … letting go of any tension in the gut … stress that you hold here seems to melt away … disappearing as each moment passes by … allow it to go ….

(pause)

your stomach is so very relaxed … calm. soothed … in a state of automatic flow… feeling appreciation for this nice sensation in your abdomen ….

(pause)

as you follow along with your breath … allow for this comforting feeling to travel up into your ribs and chest … deeply relaxing your heart … imagine you can focus directly on your heart … this strong muscle beats kindly for you … it deserves to relax … it deserves your love …. send your heart love right now in whatever way feels best for you …

(pause)

Good…

witness your lungs gently expanding and contracting with the breath …. allow this sensation to relax you even more ….

(pause)

Now imagine that this beautiful sensation of relaxation is slowly traveling down each arm… melting away any tension as it moves ever so slowly…

(pause)

Feel this profound comfort from the neck down… you are almost fully immersed in deep relaxation…

(pause)

You are ready to allow this wonderful feeling to slowly travel up your neck now, relaxing any tension that may be present in the jaw… and cheeks… and mouth… and nose… feel your eyes even relaxing behind the eyelids… you deserve this…

(pause)

Let your entire forehead feel as if it is melting away all the years of anxiety or stress…. Let it all go…

(pause)

You are doing so well…

(pause)

Right now, this time is fully for you… time for you to let go and feel a deep state of relaxation… the perfect amount of comfort that is right for you in this very moment… allow it…

(pause)

By now, your entire head is so very relaxed… laying heavy upon a pillow… resting…

(pause)

On the count of three, send a signal to all of your muscles in the body to let go of any last remaining tension… you can do this…

1…. 2…. 3….

Let any stress or pressure release…. Returning to your natural state of balance…

(pause)

You may be feeling a soothing heaviness…. Or a gentle lightness… whatever you are feeling is right for you… experience it… allow it… enjoy it…

(pause)

It is impossible for anxiety to be present in this deep state of relaxation you have cultivated, so really soak up the feeling of being perfectly balanced… aligned with how you truly are meant to feel…

(pause)

Right now,… right here… you are relaxed… you have no where to be and nothing to do… no one needs you and you don't need to do anything… simply rest…

(pause)

This deep state of relaxation allows for any healing to take place on a cellular level, so please tune in to the great power of natural regeneration…

(pause)

All of your body's systems are in perfect working order… your body is working as a unit… all is well… all is sound…

(pause)

Your mind is free to roam through thoughts as they pass on by… your emotions calm and tuned into the perfect state of being…

(pause)

Relax…

(pause)

Now, if you'd like you can imagine something that brings you fear, but since you are in such a wonderful state of calm, you can witness this fear without getting emotionally involved… what is it that commonly makes you afraid? Just see it, as if you are watching a black and white movie…

(pause)

See this fear on a screen in front of you… the movie is called "something that holds me back"

Fear is simply a signal that you are being presented with something you need to overcome in order to be truly free and happy…

(pause)

What is it that stops you from being your best?

(pause)

As the movie plays through, you are shown what life would be like if you stepped through this fear and made it safely to the other side… notice how the movie flushes out into full and vibrant color…

(pause)

What are you doing in this beautiful movie now that you are on the other side of what held you back?

(pause)

See the movie in radiant colors and magnificent scenes that show you living out your dreams… you are successful… you are glowing with good health… you are amazing… hear all the sounds…

(pause)

Now, imagine that you can step directly into this movie and actually FEEL how it is on the other side of fear…

(pause)

Touch something in your surroundings…. Witness the people who are around… see if you can smell any fragrances… what kinds of clothes do you wear when you are free from fear?

(pause)

Very good…

Breathe in very deeply once more, and say to yourself "I am determined to make this my reality"

And begin drawing your awareness to the present moment… feeling confident… calm… and a boost in self-esteem that you can overcome anything…

Wiggle your fingers to become aware of your body… open your eyes to reorient yourself to the room… you did it… welcome back.

Chapter 26
30 Minute Guided Meditation for Sleep, Relaxation, & Stress Relief

[Introduction- Stretch and positioning: 3 minutes]

Prepare your room by turning off any devices that might be a distraction. You may need to put your phone in another room if you are tempted to check it repeatedly. Turn off the TV or any music that is playing. You want to set the stage for a night of rest and relaxation. Dim the lights.

Lie down, on your back and settle into a position that is comfortable for you. If you are not comfortable lying on your back, you might want to put a or rolled blanket under your knees. Make sure that your head and neck are supported as well.

If it is comfortable for you, try moving your head back and forth and turning it side to side to loosen up your neck muscles.

Let it relax back into a comfortable position

Wiggle your shoulders and let them fall back into a relaxed position

Keeping your buttocks on the bed, move your hips a bit and then let them fall back into a relaxed position.

You want your body to be in a neutral and comfortable position so:

Make sure that your chin is not pointing too far up. Tuck in in just a bit to allow the neck to lengthen and the jaw to relax.

Tuck your shoulders underneath you and then let them relax into a natural position

Let your hands rest at your sides, palms up or down, or on your abdomen.

Let your legs relax, your feet and knees may roll out when they are relaxed. Try not to hold them in any specific position, just let them fall naturally.

Pause to allow participants a couple minutes to adopt a comfortable position.

[Intention Setting And Focus On Breathing: 10 Minutes]

You may find that you will doze during this meditation. That is ok. Don't force yourself to stay awake if you feel that you are sleepy.

Close your eyes lightly. For this time, you aren't going to try to do anything. There is no need to worry about things that happened today or things that might happen tomorrow. Right now, all you need to do is to be here, in your body, on your bed letting your mind do what it needs to do to relax for a good night's sleep.

Thank yourself for taking this time for self-care. You deserve a night of restful sleep and to wake up feeling refreshed and ready for the day. This is one thing that you can do that is just for yourself. No guilt, no worries.

Know that whatever worries you and stops you from sleeping won't be fixed by keeping you awake.

Know that no matter how you slept last night, or the night before, you can sleep well tonight. This is the only night that matters.

Pause a minute for reflection

Breath in and out naturally a few times.

Pause a minute for reflection

Take a few deep breaths and exhale whatever tension you feel. Inhale slowly and really feel where the air is going. It is normal to breath less than we can. Right in this moment, you want to breath as fully as possible.

Take a deep breath and feel the air as it flows through your nostrils, down into your lungs and fully into your abdomen. Breathe in as deeply as you can.

Exhale slowly, pushing the air out, first from your abdomen and then from your lungs.

Think about any areas of tightness you may have had when you took that breath. If it felt stuck anywhere, feel what it would be like to relax that area.

You are going to take a few deep breaths again and think about relaxing into the breath. I will be giving you instructions for relaxation but don't feel that you need to match the pace of your breath with my instructions. Just keep breathing deeply and try to apply the instructions with each breath.

When you exhale, don't push out the air so much that you are pulling in your stomach.

On your next deep inhale, feel the flow through your nostrils, down behind your jaw into your throat. Sometimes people tighten their throat when breathing deeply. Try to tuck your chin, just a bit, to lengthen your neck relax your jaw and think about opening your throat to allow the air to pass freely through and into your lungs.

Exhale slowly, feeling the air flow out of your body.

Pause a minute for reflection

Exhale naturally.

Pause a minute for reflection

On your next deep inhale, feel the airflow from your nostril, down your throat and into your lungs. Feel your abdomen rise as you fill your lungs. Relax your stomach and let it push out. Don't worry, no one is watching. Use your stomach to help your lungs fill more fully. A lot of us aren't used to relaxing our stomachs this way. We don't like to push it out and look fat but know that no one is watching you right now.

Exhale naturally, relax your stomach and try that again. Inhale deeply, feeling the air in your lungs and your abdomen pushing out. Relaxing your shoulders and letting your stomach push out.

Take three more deep breaths at your own pace, feel for any remaining areas of tension. Meet those areas without judgment and try to relax them. Don't worry if they still feel tight. Just take note of them as you move your attention elsewhere.

Let your breath relax and become natural again.

Pause a minute for reflection

[Body Scan: 10 Minutes]

As your body relaxes, it may begin to feel heavy. Feel how it rests on the bed. You are supported in this meditation by the things around you. They hold you and allow you to do the work you need to do to unclutter your mind.

Like your breath, your body may hold areas of tension that distract you. As we scan the body, we will try to release these areas and achieve a fuller relaxation. When you notice tension, try to relax those muscles. You may find that a small stretch and release of the muscles helps reduce the tension. This doesn’t have to be a big movement. It is something that resets the muscle memory into one of relaxation rather than tension.

Bring your attention to the top of your head. Focus on what that feels like. Maybe it's warm or maybe you feel a breeze. If you don't think about it much, it might be hard to feel the top of your head. Imagine it touching the air around you. You might feel something strongly, like heat or a breeze. Whatever you feel, or don't feel, is ok. Just notice whatever it is, without judgment.

Pause a minute for reflection

Move your attention to your cheeks and around your mouth. Notice if you are holding tension in either of these places. Think about what to would feel like to let that tension go. Try bringing your lips into a soft small smile. This smile is mostly internal. It always feels better to smile and helps to relax your whole face. Don't worry if this all feels a little funny, just relax and let it happen or not without judgment.

Pause a minute for reflection

Now bring your attention to your neck and shoulders. These are very common areas for storing stress and tension. If you keep them tight, you may not even be able to imagine what they would feel like relaxed. Try shrugging your shoulders and tucking them back. Move your head back and forth a little bit. If any of these actions hurts, stop. Let your shoulders feel heavy and fall away from your neck. Notice whatever you feel in your neck and shoulders without judgment. However much you relax them is more than they were relaxed before!

Pause a minute for reflection

Focus on your heart area, stomach, and abdomen. Notice if you are holding any tension on those areas. Nerves and worries like to settle there. You can let those go for now. You have already promised yourself that you will get to those things when you are finished with this. You can let the wait for just a few more minutes while you prepare your mind for them. Holding tension in your stomach won't help them to get done. Try to imagine your chest and stomach relaxed and not distracting you from things you want to focus on.

Pause a minute for reflection

Move your attention to your arms. They might feel heavy to you, that is how they are when they are relaxed. Let them rest however is comfortable to you. Notice if you have any tension in your hands and stretch your fingers just a bit to let that go. Let them relax again, resting on your legs or the floor.

Pause a minute for reflection

Bring your attention into your lower back and pelvis. You've been sitting still for a few minutes and may find that you are tight. Feel free to wiggle a bit to get comfortable and release any tension that may be in your lower back. Notice any areas of tension in your pelvis. Let any tension go without letting yourself slump or slouch.

Pause a minute for reflection

Now move your attention to your legs and feet. Sometimes, we are so used to holding ourselves up with our legs that we don't even notice the tension we have in our thighs. Lt the fall naturally while keeping your feet connected to the floor. If you are lying down, let your knees and feet fall naturally to the side. You may want to stretch or wiggle them a bit to feel the relaxation.

Take three deep breaths at your own pace, linger a bit on the exhale but don't force it.

Feel what this state of full relaxation feels like. Maybe you haven't felt this relaxed in a while. Know that you can create this for yourself at any time.

Pause for moment for reflection

[Conclusion: 7 Minutes]

Shift your focus back to your breath. Let your breathing become natural and notice the inhale and exhale. Try not to force it. If you find yourself breathing slower or faster than normal, notice that and try to let the need to control the breath go. Normally, you don't think much about your breathing so it's common for people to change how they breathe when they start to pay attention to it.

This is a light focus on your breath.

It's just in …. And out….

One breath, in…. And out

When your mind drifts, notice that you have become distracted and, without judging, bring your attention back to this one breath.

Focus on just this breath….

Take each breath one at a time.

Pause for a couple minutes of silence.

As you end this meditation, thank yourself for taking this time to prepare yourself and settle your mind and body for a restful night's sleep. It might not feel like it, but you have taken an important step towards clearing your mind and practicing relaxation. This will help you to let go of whatever thoughts or worries might prevent you for sleeping well.

Know that you can achieve this level of relaxation every night before bed. When you want this, just take a moment to feel your breath and remind yourself that worries, and tension are just distractions that you can put aside while you focus on more important things. Whenever you feel them creeping into your mind, bring your attention back to the breath.

Inhale

Exhale

Take one more deep breath and feel the weight of your body on the bed. This is rest. This is how you replenish.

Let yourself feel this fully and completely

Let yourself rest.

Chapter 27

Guided Meditation for Anxiety

Find a comfortable place to sit. Either on a chair or on the ground.

Adjust your posture accordingly and sit upright with your spine straight, neck tall and shoulders relaxed.

When you are ready, gently close your eyes.

Allow yourself to settle in the here and now.

(10 seconds)

Become aware of your surroundings. Notice any sounds around you. They may be loud or subtle. Maybe there is a sound of the clock ticking. Or, the humming noise of your air conditioning. Or, noise from the streets. Maybe you can hear the chirping of the birds outside. Or, it is completely silent. Just notice whatever sounds or silence in your environment.

(20 seconds)

Now, pay attention to your thoughts and notice what thoughts are popping up in your mind

(5 seconds)

What are you thinking about?

Are you thinking of your problems or your plans for the day?

Just become aware of the thoughts in your mind and let them go.

(10 seconds)

Now, bring your attention to your breathing.

Take a deep breath in through your nose and feel it fill your body.

(5 seconds)

Exhale completely and let the air leave your body.

(5 seconds)

Keep breathing deeply.

(30 seconds)

When you notice your mind wandering, just focus on your breathing and bring your attention back to my voice.

(30 seconds)

Feel the sensation in your nose as the air touches it.

(15 seconds)

Become aware of the air as it fills your lungs till they are fully inflated.

(5 seconds)

Then, gently release your breath and feel as your lungs become deflated. Feel the air leave your body through the nose.

(5 Seconds)

Now, return to your normal breathing rhythm. Let your breathing assume its own natural rhythm and just observe each inhale and exhale.

(30 seconds)

Remain alert and aware. If your mind wanders, bring your attention back to your breathing.

(30 seconds)

Now, notice the parts of your body that are in contact with the ground. Fell the support of the surface beneath you.

(10 seconds)

Direct your focus to your toes. Wiggle all your ten toes and feel them relaxing.

(10 seconds)

Make circles with your feet and let your ankles relax.

(10 seconds)

Notice your calf muscles and knees. Tighten the muscles around them and let go.

(10 seconds)

Bring your attention to your thighs, squeeze them together and release allowing them to relax.

(10 seconds)

Take your attention to your buttocks and feel them pressing down the surface beneath you. Relax them and let go of any tension around them.

(10 seconds)

Focus on your pelvic area and relax it.

(10 seconds)

Move your attention to your back. Do you feel any tension?

Tighten the muscles in your back and release them. Feel them relax as the tension around your back dissolves away.

(10 seconds)

Gently, take a deep breath through your nose and feel the air fill your entire body and then exhale completely releasing it.

(10 seconds)

Take a deep breath in and fill your belly completely allowing it to expand as much as possible and then exhale letting it fall and completely relax.

(10 seconds)

Round your shoulders and upper back and squeeze your chest muscles and then release and assume an upright position allowing the chest to open au.

(10 seconds)

Now, bring your attention to the shoulders. Squeeze them up towards your ears and then release them down letting go any tension as you feel them relax.

(10 seconds)

Stretch out your hands in front of you and make tight fists and then release spreading your fingers wide.

(10 seconds)

Rets your hands on your lap.

Drop your chin towards your collar bone and let the back of your neck stretch and release and tension.

(10 seconds)

Lift your chin as up as possible and allow the front of your neck to stretch and release tension.

(10 seconds)

Clench your jaw, close your eyes and tighten your facial muscles. Breath in deeply and hold your breath in for 7,6,5,4,3,2,1 and exhale gently as you allow your jaw and facial muscles to relax and then open your eyes.

(10 seconds)

Sit in the awareness of your entire body. It is relaxed and alert.

(30 seconds)

Bring back your attention to your breathing.

Inhale deeply and silently repeat the mantra 'I am inhaling.'

Exhale slowly as you silently say to yourself, 'I am exhaling.'

Keep breathing and reciting the mantras "I am inhaling", "I am exhaling".

(30 seconds)

When you notice your mind wandering, gently bring you attention back to your breathing and repeat the mantra.

I am inhaling.

I am exhaling

(30 seconds)

Gently direct your awareness to your body.

Feel the surface you are sitting on.

(5 seconds)

Notice the temperature on your skin.

(5 seconds)

Listen to the sounds around you.

(5 seconds)

Listen to your breathing.

(5 seconds)

Notice the sensations in your body.

(5 seconds)

Gently wiggle your fingers and your toes.

When you feel ready, open your eyes.

You are now ready to go on with your plans for the rest of the day.

Quick Guided Meditation For Anxiety

Sit comfortably in your chair and relax.

Gently close your eyes and begin to become aware of your breath. Bring your attention to your nose and notice the air as it comes in and goes out.

(20 seconds)

Take a deep breath in and release it slowly.

Take three more deep breaths.

(30 seconds)

Allow your body to relax and adapt to your breathing rhythm.

10 seconds

Notice the sounds in and out of the room; These sounds are not distractions but simply an expression of what is happening in your surroundings. Notice them and continue to breathe deeply and let your body continue to relax.

(30 seconds)

Is your mind wandering? It is okay for your mind to move from one thought to another. Slowly, focus your attention back to your breath. Notice how your chest is rising as you breathe in and gently falling as you breath out.

(20 seconds)

Make each inhale deep until your lungs cannot accommodate any more air.

(10 seconds)

And then breathe out completely allowing all the air out.

(10 seconds)

Keep focusing on your breathing, and if you feel your mind wandering gently guide it back to your breathing.

(30 seconds)

Breath in deeply.

Breath out gently.

Release all the expectations that you are holding on for this practice.

(10 seconds)

Your only responsibility at this moment is to consciously breath in and slowly release your breath.

Let go of all the judgments that you hold on this meditation. About whether you are being perfect or not.

(10 seconds)

As you breathe in notice your belly rises and as your breath out slowly notice the belly fall.

(20 seconds)

Allow yourself to relax and be present to this moment.

(30 seconds)

Now, take three deep breaths.

(30 seconds)

When you are ready, gently open your eyes and move your body slowly.

Chapter 28

Guided Meditation for Anxiety and Stress

Try to practice this exercise daily,

in a place where nobody is going to

disturb you.

During this exercise I'm going to ask you

to contract your muscles but this

shouldn't be something uncomfortable or painful.

As I direct you, try to contract

your muscles up to 60 to 70 percent of

your capacity.

Also, keep in mind that is

completely normal if your mind loses

focus or you get distracted.

If any thoughts come to your mind,

simply watch them without any judgment.

Some people are not used to being relaxed

and they may think this is just a waste of time,

but achieving mastery of the art of

relaxation is a very important element

to get rid of anxiety and stress.

If you find it difficult to relax, that is a

very powerful reason to practice this

exercise more often.

As with any other discipline,

the more you practice it,

the better you get at it and the more

you're going to be able to enjoy it.

This is very critical to achieve the results you

want, so let's begin…

Put yourself in a comfortable position.

You might be sitting on a chair or a

couch… a place that gives support to your

back, where you can keep your back

straight.

Or if you want to do it laying on your bed,

it's perfectly fine. Just feel comfortable.

Now I invite you to close your eyes and begin

bringing your attention to your breath.

Notice when you inhale and when

you exhale.

Breathe deeply and slowly through your

Nose.

Try to breathe filling up your belly

with air and then let it go.

Put your focus on filling your belly with

air and exhale letting go of any tension.

If you find it easier, you can put your

hand on top of your belly and feel your

hand going up when you breathe in and going down when you breathe out.

Notice how the fresh air feels when it

goes through your nose and goes inside

your body.

Notice how your belly moves as you

inhale and exhale.

Every time you breathe out, let go of any

Tension.

With every breath you take, you get more and more relaxed.

Continue to bring your attention to your

breath. Take a deep breath slowly.

Hold the air for a second and slowly breathe out letting go of any tension.

Take another deep breath.

Hold the air and slowly let it go let go any stress

and tension.

Take another deep breath.

Hold the air and breathe out letting go any accumulated tension in your body, in your mind.

Now bring your attention to your

Feet. Notice how they feel.

Are they warm?

Are they cold?

Or heavy?

Do you feel any tingling?

And whenever you're ready, start to

contract and tense the muscles of your

feet.

Feel the tension for a few moments

and then relax the tension.

Relax your feet and your toes.

With every breath,

relax your feet more and more.

Now bring your attention to your legs.

Bring your attention to your ankles, your

Knees, your thighs…

All your legs.

Pay attention to any sensation

that you might be feeling on your legs

and whenever you're ready,

contract and tense the muscles of your

legs.

Sustain the tension, maintain the

contraction.

And now, let it go slowly.

Invite your legs to relax.

Take a deep breath

and allow yourself to experience more

and more relaxation as you breathe.

Now bring your attention

to the muscles of your pelvis and your

back.

Pay attention to any tension that

is present in this area,

identify any tension

and whenever you are ready start to

contract the muscles of your buttocks,

by pressing them tightly.

Arch your back up and away from the floor or chair.

Pay attention to these sensations of

tension as you contract your muscles…

[wait a few seconds]

and then relax those muscles.

Relax any tension.

Breathe out and let go of any tension.

Now bring your attention to your

shoulders and your neck. Notice if you

are experiencing any tension

in this area.

Notice how it feels

and what sensations you may experience

around this area.

Whenever you're ready, contract and tense the muscles of your shoulders and your neck.

Press the back of your head

against the chair or your bed.

Now shrug your shoulders.

Just try to lift your shoulders to

your ears and bring your chin as

close as you can to your chest.

Sustain the tension and pay attention to any sensation that you are experiencing

right now, …

Now relax and let go the tension on

your shoulders and your neck.

With every breath you take, relax your

shoulders and your neck more and more.

Now bring your attention to your hands

and your arms. Notice how they feel.

Are they warm?

Are they cold?

Heavy?

Do you feel any tingling?

Pay attention to those sensations.

Take a deep and a slow breath

and whenever you're ready, start to

contract those muscles.

Lift your arms in front of you.

Contract your hands, clench them,

making a fist and

bend your hands back at the wrist.

Feel the tension in your arms for a few

moments.

Slowly let the tension go

and allow your hands and your arms to

relax. Let them rest.

Take a deep breath

and as you breathe out, let go of any

tension that may have remained in your

arms.

Now bring your attention to your face

and your head. Notice any sensation in

your lips, in your cheeks, in your eyelids,

your nose, in your forehead and your skull.

Continue to breathe slowly and

deeply as you pay attention and try to

identify any sensation in your face and

your head…

And whenever you're ready, begin

to contract and tense those muscles

closing your eyes firmly, lift your eyebrows as much as you can.

Press your lips together tightly and extend your lips pulling them outward.

Tense every muscle in your face.

Feel and experience any sensation of

tension in your face or your head, and

whenever you're ready… relax!

Relax all those muscles.

As you relax those muscles

You may open your mouth slightly and

continue to relax all the other muscles

in your face.

Notice the difference between

the state of tension and

relaxation.

Now bring your attention back to your

Breath. Make sure you're breathing deeply and slowly and allow yourself to relax more and more, letting go of any tension.

Now I'm going to invite you to scan your

whole body and try to find any source of

tension that may have remained.

Start by your feet.

Check on your legs, your back, your pelvis.

Continue scanning your shoulders,

your arms. Check your neck,

your face and your head.

Pay attention to the feeling of relaxation

and let go of any tension

that you may have found now.

Bring your attention back to your breath

and enjoy the feeling of relaxation all

around your body.

Keep enjoying it. Enjoy

all these for as long as you want

And whenever you're ready,

without any rush, start moving

your toes, your fingers and bring back

your attention to the place where you

are.

You can open your eyes and stay in a

state of total peace and relaxation.

As I already mentioned, try to practice this exercise more often. Ideally every day at least once a day to maximize its benefits.

Also, I would like to ask you if you can please leave a comment about how your experience with this exercise has been.

Chapter 29

Guided Chakra Meditation for Anxiety and Stress Relief

Find a comfortable position either seated or lying down and gently close your eyes.

(5 seconds)

Become aware of your surroundings. Are there any sounds in your immediate environment?

(5 seconds)

Is it warm or cold? Is the air humid?

(5 seconds)

The air you are breathing is it warm or cold? Does it have a smell, or it is odorless?

(5 seconds)

Now, become aware of the parts of your body that are in contact with the ground. Allow your body to become limp and for the surface beneath you to support you.

(10 seconds)

Notice any sensations on your skin.

(10 seconds)

Notice any sensations on the different parts of your body.

(10 seconds)

Begin to take deep breaths.

(20 seconds)

Let the inhales and exhales allow you relax.

(20 seconds)

Notice as your chest rise and fall with every inhale and exhale.

(10 seconds)

Feel the sensation in your nostrils as you breathe in and out.

(10 seconds)

Become aware of the difference in temperature of the air that you are inhaling and the one that you are exhaling.

(20 seconds)

Now bring your attention to your tailbone, the bottom of your spine where the root chakra is located. Visualize a red circle of energy pulsating on the area around your tailbone. Take some deep breaths and visualize the energy going to your root chakra, easing any tension held on this part of your body

(30 seconds)

This root chakra is responsible for connecting you to the energy of the earth. When your root chakra is balanced, you feel grounded and supported. On the other hand, when your root chakra is overactive, you feel jittery and anxious. It might also manifest physically as digestive problems, lower back pain, hip pain, ovarian issues and prostate issues in men.

To balance your root chakra every day, incorporate grounding activities such as meditating and prayer in your everyday life. Also spend time in nature.

(10 seconds)

Repeat the following mantras to help you get grounded:

"I am here."

(5 seconds)

"I deserve to be here."

(5 seconds)

“The Earth is my support.”

(5 seconds)

Take a few deep breaths here as you pay attention to the surface beneath you.

(30 seconds)

Now bring your attention to the area just below the belly button where your sacral chakra is located. Visualize an orange circle of energy pulsating around this area. Take some deep breaths and visualize the energy going to your sacral chakra, easing any tension held on this part of your body

(30 seconds)

This sacral chakra is responsible for your creative and sexual energy. When your sacral chakra is balanced, you feel motivated and relish in the joys of life without needing to overindulge. You are also sexually and creatively expressive. On the other hand, when your sacral chakra is overactive you have addictive and overindulgent tendencies. When it is underactive you experience a lack of passion, decreased sex drive and lack of creativity. Physically, an manifest as depression, obesity, hormonal imbalance and addiction.

To balance your sacral chakra, engage in creative activities often.

Repeat the following mantras,

"I am infinitely creative"

(5 seconds)

"It is ok for me to enjoy life"

(5 seconds)

"I let go the need to overindulge"

Take a few deep breaths as you pay attention to your sacral chakra.

(30 seconds)

Bring your attention the area on the top of your stomach where your ribs meet. This is where your solar plexus chakra is located. Visualize a yellow circle of energy pulsating around this area. Take some deep breaths and visualize the energy going to your solar plexus, easing any tension held on this part of your body

(30 seconds)

This solar plexus chakra is responsible for your sense of confidence and personal power. When your solar plexus chakra is balanced, you feel confident, a sense of wisdom, as sense of personal power and you are decisive. Otherwise, when it is underactive, you may feel timid, indecisive, insecure and needy. When it is overactive you may feel too energized, greedy, angry and have a need to control and micromanage.

Physically, in imbalanced solar plexus chakra manifests as digestive issues or issues on internal organs such as kidneys, liver, appendix and pancreas.

To balance your solar plexus chakra, recite self-esteem and self-confidence affirmations.

Repeat the following affirmation:

"I am enough"

(5 seconds)

"I am worthy"

(5 seconds)

"I am confident"

(5 seconds)

Take a few deep breaths here as you pay attention to the area around your solar plexus.

(30 seconds)

Now, move your attention to center of your chest where your heart chakra is located. Visualize a green circle of energy pulsating around this area. Take some deep breaths and visualize the energy pulsating in your chest area, easing any tension held on this part of your body

(30 seconds)

The heart chakra is responsible for your ability to give and receive love. It is also associated with compassion, kindness, empathy, joy and peace. of confidence and personal power. When your heart chakra is balanced you give and receive love with ease. You are kind and compassionate to others. When it is overactive, you may find it difficult to set healthy boundaries for yourself or you may experience interpersonal relationship issues. When it is underactive, you might find it difficult getting close to other people.

To balance your heart chakra, offer yourself self-love. Treat yourself with compassion and kindness and extend the same to other people. Engage in acts of service that are within your boundaries.

Repeat the following affirmation:

"I accept myself"

(5 seconds)

"I am willing to learn to love myself unconditionally"

(5 seconds)

"I am kind and compassionate to myself and others"

(5 seconds)

Take a few deep breaths here as you pay attention to the area around your heart center.

(30 seconds)

Now, move your attention to your throat where the throat chakra is located. Visualize a purple circle of energy pulsating around this area. Take some deep breaths and visualize the energy pulsating in your throat area, easing any tension held on this part of your body

(30 seconds)

The throat chakra is responsible for expressing your personal truth with clarity, love and kindness. If your throat chakra is overactive or interrupting others. When it is underactive, you may feel shy or opt to remain silent even on issues that are important to you. Physically, an imbalanced throat chakra may manifest as loss of voice, throat pain, cavities, or mouth ulcers

When speaking always think:

"Is it the truth?"

"Is it necessary?"

"Is it kind?"

To balance your throat chakra practice expressing your emotions and truths.

Repeat the following affirmation:

"It is ok for me to speak my truth"

(5 seconds)

"Even when I feel like my truth does not matter, I will say it anyway"

(5 seconds)

"It is becoming easier and easier for me to speak my truth"

(5 seconds)

Take a few deep breaths here as you pay attention to the area around your collarbone and throat area.

(30 seconds)

Now, move your attention to the space between your eyebrows. This is where the third crown chakra is located. Visualize an indigo circle of energy pulsating around this area. Take some deep breaths and visualize the energy pulsating on the area around you're the space between your eyebrows, easing any tension held on this part of your body

(30 seconds)

The crown chakra is responsible for intuition. It is believed to give the brain access to information that is beyond the material world and what your five senses can detect. When it is balanced you feel in tune with both yourself as well as the physical and material world. You will receive intuitive messages with ease.

When it is overactive you may become obsessed with getting psychic information. On the other hand, when it is underactive, you may feel spiritually disconnected. Physically, an imbalanced crown chakra may manifest as headaches, vision problems or sinuses.

To balance your crown chakra, spend time in nature and engage in spiritual activities regularly.

Repeat the following affirmation:

"I am tuned in to my intuition"

(5 seconds)

"I am in alignment with the universe"

(5 seconds)

"I am divinely guided"

(5 seconds)

Take a few deep breaths here as you pay attention to the area between your eyebrows.

(30 seconds)

Now, move your attention to the top of your head where your crown chakra is located. Visualize a white circle of energy pulsating around this area. Take some deep breaths and visualize the energy pulsating on the area on the top your head, easing any tension held on this part of your body.

(30 seconds)

The crown chakra is responsible for pure conscious energy. It is the center of enlightenment and spiritual connection with your higher self. When it is balanced you feel in tune with your higher self and divine consciousness. When it is underactive, you may feel spiritually disconnected. Physically, an imbalanced crown chakra may manifest as headaches.

To balance your crown chakra, engage in spiritual activities regularly and balance the other chakras.

Repeat the following affirmation:

"I am spiritual being experiencing humanness"

(5 seconds)

"I am connected to my highest self"

(5 seconds)

Take a few deep breaths here as you pay attention to the area around the crown of your head.

(30 seconds)

Once more visualize the various energy circles pulsating on all your chakras. A red circle of energy on your tailbone, orange circle of energy two inches below your belly button, a yellow circle of energy on your solar plexus, a green circle of energy on your chest, a purple circle of energy on your throat, an indigo circle of energy between your eyebrows and a white circle of energy on the crown of your head. See all the circles of energy vibrating simultaneously.

(30 seconds)

Now, bring your attention your body. Notice how your body feels and any sensations. Notice how calm, grounded and peaceful you feel and rest in this awareness.

(60 seconds)

Begin to deepen your breath.

(10 seconds)

Gently move your head from side to side.

(10 seconds)

Come to stillness and when you are ready gently open your eyes.

Chapter 30

Guided Meditation for Happiness

In this exercise, I will guide you through a simple meditation that includes breathing exercises to help you relax and focus on your breathing. This exercise includes different strategies that you can use to increase your happiness quotient. I will help you hold onto all positive thoughts and let go of all the negativity within and around you.

This meditation you to this mediation that will help you cultivate happiness.

Before I begin, find yourself something comfortable to wear and avoid any tight-fitting clothes.

You can either lie down or sit comfortably. You can sit in a chair or sit on the ground with your legs crossed. Let your hands rest one over the other in a standard meditation pose.

If you feel uncomfortable at any time, you can stop the recording.

Now, you need to close your eyes and listen to the recording.

During this time, you can release yourself from the stress and tensions of the day and from all your responsibilities, for a while at least.

Let your mind be free to explore, to smile and experience happiness.

Concentrate on your breathing and nothing else.

Feel your breaths becoming deep and long.

Take a couple of moments, breathe in and breathe out, allow yourself to let go of the world outside

Start to visualize a path in your mind. The path can be anything that you want it to be, but at the end of it, you need to be able to see a door. This door opens up the path to your inner world. Now, open the door and you can see a ray of bright light. The light is warm, welcoming, and helps you to relax.

You can see the bright inner world of yours and you need to step into this beautiful world.

Relax into all the warmth and harmony existing within.

You are the only one that knows this place and you are the only one with the key to open up this world.

Take a deep breath and shut the door to the outer world.

Give yourself the permission to enter this place and fully immerse yourself into this world of inner peace. It is a world where you feel safe and you can experience happiness here.

Give yourself this time to work on your happiness so that it spreads joy within your body and eventually radiates from you.

It is okay even if your mind wanders. It is perfectly alright even if you realize that your thoughts have gone off tangent.

You are in charge of your thoughts and if you feel like your thoughts are wandering, you can bring awareness back. Listen to the sound of my voice and concentrate on my voice.

Now, take a deep breath.

Start with your feet; feel your toes relax and then feel your feet relax.

Feel your legs relax slowly.

Feel the muscles in your thigh loosen and then the muscles in your abdomen relax.

Gently will them to relax.

Shift your focus towards your chest. Will the muscles around your ribcage to relax, then move onto your back?

You can now feel the muscles in your shoulders relax and all the tension starts to fade away.

Now, allow the muscles in your neck to relax and move towards your head.

Take a deep breath and allow your entire body to relax.

Your breath fills up your lungs with air.

Start to exhale slowly until there is no air in your lungs.

Take a deep breath to fill your lungs with air. Allow your lungs to expand and once they do, breathe out.

Breathe in through your nose for a count of four.

One, two, three and four.

Hold your breath.

Exhale through your mouth for a count of eight.

One, two, three, four, five, six, seven and eight.

Breathe in again. One, two, three and four.

Breathe out. One, two, three, four, five, six, seven, and eight.

Visualize the path that you took to enter your inner world.

Walk on the same path and the same bright light that you saw now surrounds you.

Walk on the path that leads you through an alpine forest.

There are white pine trees that line the path.

The morning sun is shining brightly and is casting soft golden rays of warm sunlight all around you.

Continue to walk on this path and you will find a rock outcrop overlooking a landscape of mountains.

There are hundreds of peaks all around you; some seem closer than the others.

Let your gaze take in the expanse of mountains in front of you and you will feel a feeling of peace wash over you.

Appreciate the beauty of nature that's all around you. Revel in this gift and be thankful for it.

Enjoy the view and give yourself a moment to smile. Smile at the beauty that's present in front of you.

The golden rays of sunlight are illuminating the landscape. The colors are gently mixing with each other all around you and it looks like a beautiful painting.

Smile and become aware of all the flora and fauna around you.

Imagine the sounds of birds chirping happily and smile.

Now, you will notice a large tree near you. The tree is quite old, and its trunk looks large.

Now, visualize this tree in detail. The bark of the tree looks like that of a sweet birch; its leaves smell sweet.

A gentle wind is blowing, and it blows a couple of leaves away from the tree. One such leaf lands in your hand and you smile as the leaf leaves a slight sweet-smelling minty scent.

Smile at this marvel of nature and take a deep breath.

There is something else besides the wonderful aroma. The leaves start to gently rustle and it sounds like a stringed dulcimer.

Light and airy sounds surround you.

Everything sounds melodious and they complement the wonderful landscape around you.

You are now surrounded by the warm golden light and the wonderful sounds.

Listen to the music of nature; you can feel your heart fill up with joy. There is so much beauty around you and it makes you feel happy.

Look around; there is a bush with emerald leaves next to the tree. The leaves have triangular points and the bush is filled with small berries like raspberries. Go ahead, pick a few berries and eat them.

Enjoy the flavors of these berries and savor how wonderful they feel in your mouth.

Start to slowly chew and swallow these delicious berries.

You can feel warmth and energy radiate from your core as these berries slide down your throat and into your stomach.

You can feel the energy rise within you.

This energy spreads from your stomach to your head, arms and legs. This energy is now pulsing through your body.

All your senses feel ecstatic. You feel a sense of calm and appreciation wash over you as you enjoy this wonderful bounty.

Look at the bush, the old tree, and the landscape around you.

The sun is higher in the sky and the landscape looks more beautiful than ever.

There are more wonderful scents all around you.

Allow yourself to enjoy the richness of nature and let your body soak it all up. This powerful energy continues to radiate through your body and it is casting a light halo all around you.

You can see a golden aura emanating from your body.

A pure energy makes you smile.

Bask in this wonderful energy. Let it wash over every muscle, bone, and cell of your being. Let your body be infused with nature's wonderful energy.

Stay in this place for a couple of moments and smile some more.

Now that your body is infused with this wonderful energy, it is time for you to return to the outer world.

Your inner world has given you the tools that you need to return to your day feeling energized, refreshed, and happy.

The beautiful landscape looks more golden than ever because of your aura. You feel strong and happy.

Smile more widely and you can feel this energy shine brighter. Let the sense of gratitude and appreciation wash all over you.

Whenever you feel low or dull, you can return to this place.

It is time for you to turn and go, but the sound of nature makes you linger for a while longer.

Take a deep breath and bid adieu to this wonderful place, for now.

Slowly, start to walk back up the path through which you entered. Allow yourself to soak up all the energy that this place emits. Let this energy make you feel alive.

You feel good about yourself and you are looking forward to going back to your world.

As you walk, you will notice the door to the outer world. Slowly open the door, take a deep breath, and step inside.

You are now back in the real world and you are full of happiness and positivity.

Now, breathe in slowly and deeply.

Take a deep breath through your nose and hold it for a count of four.

One, two, three and four.

Now, breathe out through your mouth and hold it to the count of eight.

One, two, three, four, five, six, seven and eight.

Take another deep breath through your nose and exhale through your mouth.

Start to slowly open your eyes and you can feel the energy of the inner world shine brightly in your body.

Take a deep breath, smile and return to your day.

You can follow this exercise whenever you want a burst of happiness. It will help you to appreciate all that is good in your life and let go of your worries.

Chapter 31
Meditation to Fall Asleep Instantly

This final meditation in this set is one that is going to help you fall asleep instantly. It is a quicker and shorter meditation that will take you through the visualization exercise.

This process makes it easier for your mindset to go from one where you might be thinking of specific things in your life to a place where you can get into a more dreamlike trance. You will be able to easily fall asleep and get that deep rest you need in order to conquer the day tomorrow. Again, ensure that you are in a comfortable place where you will be able to fall asleep for several hours at a time. This is best at night but if you plan on taking a rather long nap you could do this as well. Keep an open mind and focus on your breathing.

Meditation For A Deep And Quick Sleep

Sleep is incredibly important, but sometimes falling asleep can be difficult if we are not in the right mindset.

For this activity, we are going to take you through a visualization that will help ensure that you can get a deep sleep. It's important before falling asleep to relax your mind so that you can travel gently throughout your brain.

Start off by noticing your breath. Breathe in through your nose and out through your mouth. This is going to help calm you down so that you are able to breathe easier.

Begin by breathing in for five and out for five as we count down from twenty. Once we reach one, your mind will be completely clear. Each time a thought passes in, you will think of nothing. You will have nothing in your sight, and you will only think with your mind.

Make sure that you are in a comfortable place where you can sink into the space around you. Let your body become heavy as it falls into the bed. Keep your eyes closed and see nothing in front of you but darkness.

Each time a thought comes in, keep pushing it away. Breathe in through your nose and out through your mouth.

Remember to breathe in for five and out for five. Keep an empty mind and be ready to travel through a journey that will take you to a restful place.

You see nothing in front of you, it is completely dark, and you feel your body lifting gently up like a feather. You are light against the bed, and nothing is keeping you down. Continue to feel your body rise higher and higher. You are floating in space. There's black nothingness around you. You are gently drifting around.

You can see a few stars dotting the sky so far away, but for the most part, you see nothing. You feel yourself slowly moving through space. Your body is light and free, and nothing is keeping you strapped down. You're not afraid in this moment.

You are simply feeling easy and free. Breathe in and out, in and out.

You start to drift more towards a few planets, throughout your journey in space. You can really see now that you are up in the highest parts of the galaxy. You see out of the corner of your eye that you can actually catch a glimpse of Earth. You start gently floating towards it, having to put no effort in at all as your body is like a space rock floating through the stars.

Nothing is holding you down.

Nothing is violently pushing you either. Everything that you feel is a gentle and free emotion. You get closer and closer to Earth now and can see all the clouds that surround you. You start to move down, and you gently enter into the cloud area. Normally gravity would pull you down so fast, but right now you're just simply a gentle body drifting through the air. You get closer and closer to the land. You can see some birds here and there and a few cars and lights on the ground beneath you.

You pass all of this. Gently floating over a sleepy town.

Look down and let your mind explore what is it that you see down there. What is it that is in front of your eyes? What do you notice about this world around you as you continue to go closer and closer to home?

You are gently drifting throughout the sky. You can see trees beneath you. Now, if you reached your hand down, you'd even be able to gently feel a few leaves on the tops of the tallest trees. You don't do this now because you're just concerned with continuing to float through the sky. That's all that you really care about in this moment.

You're getting closer and closer and closer to home now, almost ready to fall asleep. You start to see that there is a lake.

You gently float down to the surface of the lake, and you land right in a boat. Your body is a little bit heavier now. You feel it relax into the bottom of the boat. Nothing around you is concerning you right now. You feel no stress or tension in any part of your body. You are simply floating through this space now.

The boat starts to gently drift on the lake. It is dark out now and you look up and see all the stars in the sky. All of this reminds you of the place that you were just a few moments ago. You start to drift closer and closer to sleep.

Do you feel as the tension leaves your body? You are peaceful throughout. You are not holding on to anything that causes you stress or anxiety. You are at ease in this moment. Everything feels good and you have no fear. You drift around in the water now for a little bit longer. You can see everything so clearly in this night sky. Just because it is dark does not mean that it's hard to see. The moon casts a beautiful glow over everything around you. You can feel the moon charging your skin. As you drift closer and closer to sleep, you feel almost nothing in your body now. You continue to focus on your breathing. You are safe, and you are at peace. You are calm, and you are relaxed. You feel incredible in this moment.

The boat starts to lift from the water. You feel as it gets higher above the water. You are even heavier now. Now you are completely glued to this comfortable surface as the boat starts to fly through the sky. You can look down and see that the city beneath you has drifted to sleep. You're getting closer and closer to home now. You can actually see your home beneath you. The boat gently takes you to your front door, and you float right in. No need to walk or climb stairs. You simply float in and straight to your bed.

You fall delicately into your bed with your head resting nicely on a pillow.

Here you are, in this moment, so peaceful and so relaxed. You are completely at ease. There's nothing that stresses you out or causes any anxiety or tension now. You are simply a body that is trying to fall asleep.

As we count down from 20, you will drift off to sleep. You will be in a very relaxed state where nothing stresses you out. You're not concerned with things that happened in the past, and you aren't going to stay up in fear of what might happen tomorrow, you are asleep. You are relaxed.

Breathe in and out. Breathe in and out.

Conclusion

These meditations are going to be an important part of a healthy sleep routine. In order to really alleviate your mind from any anxious thoughts or other things that keep you awake at night; you will want to ensure that you are calming down and becoming more relaxed before you go to bed. These meditations will be your key to becoming a happier and healthier person because of the consistent amount of rest that you'll be able to get.

The more that you practice these meditations, the easier it will be for you to get the restful sleep you deserve. You can also check out other meditations and series of books to find something with a more specific purpose, such as weight loss or positive thinking.

If you are going through a stressful time, remind yourself to gain control of your breath and that these feelings will pass. Through meditation, you have now been gifted the skill sets to help you get through just about anything whether you are dealing with anxiety, panic, or a combination of both!

If you are ever going through a rough patch, I hope you think of these meditations and take a few moments for yourself. Even if you only have several minutes, a simple breathing meditation can help put everything into perspective with you. Remember that the more you practice, the stronger your peace of mind will become. I hope that you have enjoyed learning meditation, now go forth and lead your very best life.

The key to a happy life is a happy mind and these meditations will do just that.

Meditation can bridge the gap between you and many worldly wants as well: your sleep gets better, you are able to regulate your weight, your relationships become more satisfactory and you have the ability to reduce physical pains that occasionally come and go.

Although its practice is still being blindsided by many factors, the practice is bound to receive the recognition it deserves eventually. With the internet of things, the spread of the practice is almost reaching a rampant state with the topic of meditation resting on the lips of both professionals and paupers. Even in the event that most of these people are just talking about it without putting any practice, the fact that it has gained such a massive amount of popularity is nothing but astounding. This is a positive thing though, as the positives of meditation outweigh the negatives.

For those who are a bit skeptical about engaging in it because of various reasons, I hope this serves as a beacon of light to dispel any misbeliefs and doubts one might carry about the practice. The main purpose of meditation is to reach within and access oneself. We all spend so much time on a daily basis trying to find people and things. It all falls in place easier if you discover the most important thing to find is yourself.

So, thank you once again for your kind attention. If you have found this to be useful or helpful, in any way, please tell your friends and family, or anyone whom you believe to be interested in this topic. It will surely help them find the balance they seek in life. In addition, they are surely going to benefit in the long run.

Hopefully, you now have a better understanding of how meditation can benefit you. From reading this guide, you will have gained a deeper understanding of how your mind works and how meditation alters your brain to work at its optimum. From producing the hormones and chemicals, we need to live without stress, anxiety, or depression. To be happy and balanced in our thoughts and actions.

The true test, of course, is to try it out for yourself. By this I mean really try it. Give yourself a window of time each day that you safeguard for meditation. Although it is far easier for a beginner to do this somewhere quiet and without disturbance, it will eventually be possible for you to practice meditation almost anywhere.

Make it part of your daily life, like eating, drinking, or brushing your teeth – you do brush your teeth, right? If you can make meditation habitual, then you will reap the benefits for the rest of your life.

Don't be shy about it either, spread the word, tell your friends just how awesome it is and help change someone else's life too.

People suffer in different ways, and one of the most common ways to experience pain is through anxiety. Understanding the best ways to deal with anxiety is crucial because it will enable you to deal with these issues that we face daily.

I believe that the steps outlined can help you to deal with anxiety and at the same time master how you can be in control of your life and do the things that enable you to excel and take your life to the right direction.

Start practicing these guided meditations from today, and you will see how your life will change and the positive advantages you will start experiencing once you start doing these guided meditations. Comprehending anxiety is the first step in managing it. Knowing its impulsive nature, we can get a good sense of what triggers and how our worries work - and this is where to look.

Anxiety is a state of cognition linked to an inability to control emotions. But research shows that constant feedback stimulates the brain's brain pathways, and thus enhances our ability to control emotions.

Ideally, we learn about ourselves through stressful thoughts and narratives. We learn to see, sit down and let go. In doing so, we learn two important things: ideas define us, and opinions are not real. With this new perspective, we can gradually shift our relationship to anxiety, by distinguishing between what is impossible and what is real.

Another benefit of this skill is the study of physical awareness, which teaches us to draw attention to our bodily sensations in the present moment. This technique involves examining the brain, about an inch, which makes us better aware of what we experienced physically. When exploring these emotions, you will sit with your senses in the same way as you sit with your thoughts. This new way to go can give you a safe and accessible place to go whenever stress arises

If you have been disciplined enough to follow the meditation exercises, you must have started seeing some real benefits. Although, if you follow the instructions given, you can master everything and even start doing the exercises without having to look at the instructions.

Whenever you find that you are stuck somewhere and you do not know how to go with a meditation, you can always refer to this manuscript and find what you need to do to move with the exercises smoothly.

The importance of focusing on other areas of your life is that you will maintain your goals for a long time. Therefore, I have covered these tips in this manuscript because you should not go back to where you started. The best way to achieve this goal is to ensure that all areas of your life are functioning well. When these aspects are good, you are now able to have the strength that you need to maintain the current weight that you have achieved. The concept is that you need to remain in this state for the rest of your life since this makes you enjoy your life to the fullest.

It is fair to say that this information is useful to you and many others who have considered using it in their program. As you have discovered already, meditation is a crucial tool that you can use in your daily life. Apart from that, it has helped you to achieve the goals that you desire it can also help you in other areas of your life. This means that you can keep on practicing these meditation tips as long as you find them helpful and contributing positively to the growth and development of all angles of your life. For many years, those who have discovered the many benefits that come with meditation have been doing it for various reasons. There are some who do meditation for spiritual purposes, while others do it when they are faced with a lot of stress. Although many people have found help with meditation and many have solved their problem, this does not mean that everyone can gain the same results others have gained. It largely depends on the effort that you put as an individual. Working hard will help you to achieve this, and therefore, you find that maintaining focus has been emphasized a lot in this manuscript.

What can you do if you find that you have done everything that is required for your meditation exercises, but still, you do not see any results? Truly, there are people who say that meditation is not their thing and they have tried it severally, yet it has not worked. If this is the experience you have had with the meditation exercises that we have covered in this manuscript, then you do not have to curse yourself. This may not be your problem since different people can get varying results with the mediation program they plan to use. There are other ways that are also useful, and you can use them to attain the goals you want.

Printed in Great Britain
by Amazon

55962077R00140